Thanks!
GREAT Job!

Thanks! GREAT Job!

Improve Retention, Boost Morale and Increase Engagement
with High-Value, Low-Cost Staff Recognition

Nelson Scott

EDMONTON, ALBERTA

Edited by Helen Metella
Designed by Andrew Johnstone Design
Printed in Canada

ISBN: 978-0-9877932-0-1

7243 – 112 Street
Edmonton, AB, Canada T6G 1J4
Tel: (780) 433-1443
Email: nmscott@telus.net

www.GREATstaffrecognition.com
www.seaconsultingonline.com

Library and Archives Canada Cataloguing in Publication

Scott, Nelson, 1948-
  Thanks! GREAT job! : improve retention, boost morale and increase engagement with high-value, low-cost staff recognition / Nelson Scott.

Includes bibliographical references and index.
ISBN 978-0-9877932-0-1

  1. Personnel management. 2. Employee retention. 3. Employee morale. 4. Employee motivation. 5. Labor turnover. I. Title.

HF5549.12.S46 2011   658.3'02   C2011-906418-9

Dedication

To our children Pam and Graham, whose
early employment experiences taught me
much about the importance of recognizing
staff and expressing appreciation.

In Memory

Kojak
(the dog)
1998–2010

A portion from the sale of each book will be
donated to The Rotary Foundation, the mission of
which is to advance world understanding, goodwill,
and peace through the improvement of health, the
support of education, and the alleviation of poverty.

Table of Contents

Introduction
It All Started With A Single Question

One unexpected question prompted this book. I was just wrapping up a day-long workshop called *Interview Right to Hire Right* when a participant in my audience in Grande Prairie, Alberta, lobbed it at me:

"You told us how to hire the right people, but how do we keep them? It seems like a lot of work if they just turn around and leave and we have to find someone else."

A murmur of agreement spread across the room. Others had had the same thought. Keeping people was a bigger challenge than finding them. Turnover rates were high. People were leaving so quickly—in some cases after a few days, or even hours!—that identifying the right people to hire seemed beside the point.

If they were going to invest the time to hire as I was advocating, what could be done to stop these new hires from leaving?

I don't know what my questioner expected me to say in response. Terrific pay? Extended health-care coverage? Flexible hours? On-site daycare? While all these benefits are important, I didn't refer to them in my response.

> **RECOGNITION**
>
> *Recognition is an after-the-fact display of appreciation or acknowledgement of an individual's or team's desired behavior, effort, or business result that supports the organization's goals and values.*
>
> **— Recognition Professionals International**

"Let them know that they are appreciated," I said. "Recognize them for what they achieve and how they help your organization succeed."

But what did that mean? What could managers and supervisors do to recognize staff more effectively? How could I help them do a better job?

My first step was to introduce a small section on staff recognition and retention to *Interview Right to Hire Right*. I explained the importance of keeping staff, and the financial, productivity and customer-satisfaction costs associated with high turnover. During the short time devoted to this topic, I provided a few suggestions on how to recognize staff and let them know that they are valued for who they are and what they do.

In research first conducted by Lawrence Lindahl in 1949 and replicated several times since, supervisors and workers were asked to rank 10 aspects of their jobs in order of relative importance (with 1 being high). Note the difference between what the workers and supervisors identified as most and least important in terms of on-the-job motivation.

	Supervisor's Ranking	Worker's Ranking
Good working conditions	4	9
Feeling "in" on things	10	2
Tactful disciplining	7	10
Appreciation for work done	8	1
Management loyalty to workers	6	8
Good wages	1	5
Promotion and growth opportunities	3	7
Understanding of personal problems	9	3
Job security	2	4
Interesting work	5	6

When *Briefly Noted,* the newsletter that I circulate to clients and other subscribers, first appeared in 2002, I began to write articles on staff recognition. In each issue there have always been a few high-value, low-cost staff recognition tips. I also developed a presentation on staff recognition and retention, which was followed by a second and then a third. Eventually people began to ask, "So, where's the book?"

Well, here it is!

Something that I do not write about very often—nor ever advocate—is staff recognition programs. I feel that formal programs such as service awards, employee-of-the-month programs and attendance awards are ineffective. They can be cumbersome, time consuming and expensive and they touch too few people. They do little to boost morale, increase engagement or improve retention. I will have more to say about staff recognition programs in the next chapter.

What I do advocate, for reasons that will become obvious as you read this book, is to redirect the energy and money currently consumed by ineffective programs. Let's give managers and supervisors the skills and tools they need to provide more informal, day-to-day recognition. This is the type of recognition that staff members crave most and find most meaningful.

A phrase that you will encounter repeatedly is "high-value, low-cost staff recognition." That is, high-value for recipients, but low-cost for you, in terms of the resources you have to invest: time, money and effort. The book is filled with suggestions for delivering high-value, low-cost recognition.

> "Next to physical survival, the greatest need of a human being is… to be affirmed, to be validated, to be appreciated."
> —**Stephen Covey,**
> **The Seven Habits of**
> **Highly Effective People**

As you read these tips and techniques, you will find some that you are already using successfully and others that you wish to try. Some will need to be modified to fit your organization, your budget or your personality.

A few may cause you to scratch your head. How could they possibly work? Don't feel that this reaction reflects a deficit in your understanding of staff recognition. I share your sense of bewilderment about some of these techniques. I have included ideas that I couldn't imagine using myself, but which have worked for others.

> "Recognition is acknowledgement, appreciation and achievement."
> — **Sue Glasscock & Kimberly Gram, Workplace Recognition**

The primary target audience for this book is managers and supervisors who work with front-line staff. I feel this responds to how most front-line staff—nurses, secretaries, teachers, labourers and sales associates—view the hierarchy of their organizations.

Unless they are part of the hierarchy, employees don't spend much time thinking about the CEO and her direct reports. They know they are there, but they are irrelevant to the front-line staff's day-to-day work lives. On the other hand, their direct supervisor may be the most important person in their work lives. The relationship between a supervisor, and his staff is critical to an organization's success. During exit interviews, departing employees frequently cite their relationship with their supervisor and the lack of recognition from that person, among their top reasons for leaving. Surprisingly to some, money is seldom mentioned as an important factor in the decision to leave. More people would prefer to work for a good boss for less pay than for better pay with a boss who is difficult. Staff are more likely to trust and respect managers and supervisors who are good at recognizing staff, and perceive them as effective in their jobs

Not a supervisor or manager?

Different organizations label leadership positions differently—principal, foreman, team leader, department head, superintendent, boss, owner, head nurse and so on. To keep things simple and to make the suggestions accessible to people in different industries, I have chosen to use two terms—supervisor and manager—as generic labels for all leadership roles. The only exception is when I am illustrating a point with a specific example.

Recognition and Maslow's Hierarchy of Needs

When a pipeline in North America ruptures and fuel begins to leak, people run away. In some developing countries, impoverished people rush toward the leaking pipeline. They want to capture a few litres that they can sell.

Sounds dangerous, doesn't it? It is. Every year there are reports of explosions killing people who were filling containers. Most know the dangerous consequences of their actions, but they still collect spills from the pipelines. People in developed countries wonder why.

An examination of psychologist Abraham Maslow's "hierarchy of needs"— represented by the pyramid at the bottom of this page—helps us understand what would motivate people to risk their lives for a few litres of fuel.

Maslow said that humans have an inborn order of needs that we pass through in stages. We progress to the later stages—the higher levels of the pyramid—only after our more basic needs are satisfied.

When people live in such extreme poverty that just surviving from one day to the next is a challenge, they will risk all just to survive. When satisfying their most basic needs is the priority, they don't look beyond the physiological needs to consider their own security and safety—the second level of Maslow's pyramid. Desperately poor people will take great risks to meet the basic need for food, clothing and shelter.

Certainly Canada and other developed countries have people who are living in poverty. Some are unemployed. Some are homeless or don't get enough to eat. That this occurs amidst affluence is shameful, and efforts to address their needs should be encouraged and supported.

Self-
Actualization

Self-Esteem Needs

Social Needs

Safety and Security Needs

Physiological Needs

In reality, most of the people with whom you work do not face these challenges. Having a job and receiving a regular paycheque enables them to buy food, pay the rent and clothe themselves and their families.

With a job, the need for security and safety is also addressed. They are protected from unexpected medical expenses by government health care and company benefits. Most people who have a job with a regular paycheque and benefits give little thought to their physiological and safety needs. They can begin thinking about satisfying needs higher up the pyramid.

While supervisors usually do not control pay rates and benefits, they are in a position to create work environments in which staff members can satisfy their social, esteem and self-actualization needs. After physiological and safety needs are met, the next need to be satisfied is social, which relates to belonging and being accepted. Supervisors can welcome newcomers, introduce them to co-workers and encourage interaction.

Next is the need to be valued and have a sense of contributing to the organization. By acknowledging staff members regularly for their contributions and achievements, both as individuals and members of the team, supervisors can help staff members meet their needs for self-esteem.

Finding themselves in an oppressive work environment, where criticism and negativism is common, people will shift their focus from meeting social and self-esteem needs to question whether this is the best location in which to meet physiological and safety needs. Is it time to update the resume and begin to search the help-wanted ads?

The final need—self-actualization—is related to achieving one's potential and self-fulfilment, becoming everything one is capable of becoming. Supervisors can support staff members in this pursuit by providing training and coaching to reach their potential, and challenges that require them to perform at the high level that corresponds to their capability. And they can praise them when they achieve success.

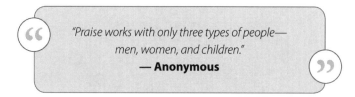

"*Praise works with only three types of people—
men, women, and children.*"
— **Anonymous**

How the Book is Organized

This book is divided into four sections:

- Why formal staff recognition programs are frequently ineffective and unnecessary
- 5 ingredients of **GREAT** staff recognition: **Genuine, Relevant, Explicit, Appropriate** and **Timely**
- Lessons—many from unlikely sources—that have shaped my thinking on staff recognition
- Tools and techniques for meaningful staff recognition that will increase engagement and productivity, boost morale and improve staff and customer retention

Throughout this book you will encounter stories of staff recognition successes and failures. Some of the stories are mine, others were told to me by others. In some cases, I have modified the details to preserve privacy.

To support my message that recognition is important, I enlisted the assistance of a variety of experts and authorities, whose words appear throughout the book. They are actually quite a diverse group: ancient philosophers, historical figures, contemporary and classical authors, business gurus, poets, cartoon characters, literary figures, religious leaders and film stars.

"Ladies and gentlemen: the story you are about to hear is true. Only the names have been changed to protect the innocent."
— Dragnet radio series, 1949 – 1957

Puhutko suomea?*

Writing this book in Finnish would have simplified it, a bit. I'm not joking. In Finnish, there is no distinction between male and female. Both "he" and "she" are covered by "hän" and "his/her" by "hänen." No clumsy constructions of "he or she" or "his/her" and "they or their" are necessary.

Alas, I can't speak, read or write Finnish. Likely, you can't either. So, I've come up with a compromise. To maintain gender neutrality I have consciously varied references to managers and employees as men or women…or should that be, "female or male?" Hopefully, I have achieved a good gender balance.

* Do you speak Finnish?

When some managers and supervisors are asked about staff recognition at my seminars, they respond with reasons for not recognizing staff. When I ask, "Why is recognition so scarce in many workplaces?" they quickly round up the usual suspects—the most common reasons for not acknowledging staff for their contributions.

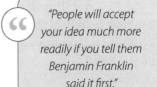

"People will accept your idea much more readily if you tell them Benjamin Franklin said it first."
— **David H. Comins, *author***

Many of these "reasons" are listed in this book, under a label that exposes them for what they truly are—excuses, rationalizations and cop-outs. They are no more valid than justifications for not exercising, for continuing to smoke, or for not following a healthy diet.

What's Up...and Down...with Staff Recognition

When we acknowledge staff and recognize them for their efforts, contributions and successes, good things happen:

Morale
is enhanced

Profits grow

Productivity rises

Staff satisfaction improves

Teamwork increases

Employee engagement improves

Recruitment becomes easier, although
there will be fewer vacancies to fill

Quality improves

Customer's satisfaction and loyalty increases

Turnover decreases

Absenteeism declines

Grumbling diminishes

Tardiness drops

The reason for recognizing staff regularly in meaningful ways is so much more compelling: It works!

Some of the conclusions in this book are based on my research and observations, as well as those of experts in the field. But don't just take our word for it. Become a do-it-yourself recognition researcher. Throughout the book, you will find suggestions for DIY Recognition Research projects. Conducting this research will add to your understanding of staff recognition and the impact it can have.

There is one last truth about a book that had a 10-year gestation period. There is much that could have been included that isn't. There just weren't enough pages. Some of the missing pieces—including recognition tips and techniques, resources and quotations—are available at www.GREATstaffrecognition.com. I invite you to visit, and while you are there, leave your own stories of staff recognition—both successes and failures.

The acronym **GREAT** reminds us of the five ingredients that make staff recognition work—recognition that improves increases engagement, boosts morale and improves retention—and most importantly, makes recognition meaningful for the recipients. For recognition to work, it must be **Genuine**. It should also be **Relevant**, **Explicit**, **Appropriate** and **Timely.**

I have devoted Section Two to these five ingredients, but for now, I will leave you with this thought:

Not all five ingredients need to be used when recognizing staff, but the presence of one is essential. Recognition must be **Genuine**. If it's not, it becomes an empty exercise. Once recognition is **Genuine,** the addition of one or more of the other components strengthens the message of appreciation.

Top 7 Reasons to Recognize Employees NOW!

1. Reduce turnover
2. Increase profitability
3. Increase productivity
4. Retain top performers
5. Create a positive work environment
6. Elevate customer service, sales and satisfaction
7. Attract a better recruiting pool

Source: Recognition Professionals International, October 29, 2008

At Least 4 Ways to Use This Book

1. This is not a whodunit. You can begin anywhere. Thumb through the book, stopping wherever something catches your eye. Jump around from chapter to chapter.

2. Abuse this book. You have my permission. Even I don't think this is great literature, or a piece of art. And it's not a textbook that you will hand on to another student for the next term. Write in it. Highlight passages. Make notes in the margins. Circle ideas you like. Cross out those you don't. Fill the book with sticky notes. If someday you would like a "clean" copy of the book, send your marked-up book back and I will replace it. No charge. Not even shipping.

3. Don't read it all at once. Look at some parts now; save other parts for later. Select a few high-value, low-cost recognition techniques to try. If they work, that's great— but you will still need to find different ways to recognize staff. As I conclude in Chapter 24, "This fat lady will never sing." Return to the book regularly or visit www.GREATstaffrecognition.com to find fresh ideas.

4. Share your book with others. Better yet (at least, from my point of view), buy them their own copies (Check out www.GREATstaffrecognition.com for quantity discounts). Discuss what you read, so that more people are focused on staff recognition. What ideas can we implement? When?

"There are two things people want more than sex and money…recognition and praise."
**— Mary Kay Ash,
businesswoman & author**

Excuses, Rationalizations and Cop-outs (Part I)

"I don't have time to recognize staff. I already have too much to do."
Granted, managers and supervisors are busy people. But we can always find time to do what we feel is important. It's a matter of setting priorities. People don't have time to acknowledge the contributions of others because they have decided that other tasks are more important than recognizing staff.

In my view, few tasks are more important than encouraging and motivating staff by acknowledging them for doing their jobs well. Staff that's well and frequently recognized will be more motivated, more productive and more focused on doing what is important. By what you recognize them for, you demonstrate which tasks and actions are **Relevant** to meeting your organization's goals successfully.

Instead of spending time with top and average performers, supervisors focus much of their time on underperformers. Instead of catching people doing good work and praising them, supervisors watch for things that go wrong that they can correct. They closely supervise these employees to ensure things don't go wrong and reprimand people when they do. When supervisors spend their days looking for what's wrong, it's hardly surprising that they don't see what's right, nor take the time to let staff know that doing what's right is appreciated.

Recognizing staff regularly will actually save you time. People who feel appreciated are less likely to look for jobs elsewhere. Low turnover means you will spend less time recruiting replacements—hours spent preparing advertising, reviewing applications, scheduling and conducting interviews, checking references, completing new-hire paperwork and orienting and training new employees.

"It's been about two months since I've worked out. I just don't have the time. Which is odd, because I have the time to go out to dinner. And watch TV. And get a bone-density test. And try to figure out what my phone number spells out in words."
— Ellen DeGeneres, TV host & actor.

"I'm not good at recognizing people. I don't know how."

If you can say, "Thank you," you already have what it takes to provide meaningful staff recognition. All we need to do is to thank people for **Relevant** contributions or achievements that assist the organization to achieve its goals. Meaningful staff recognition is no more complicated than that.

To be meaningful, recognition does not have to be formal or structured, with a series of awards reflecting different levels of achievement. Formal recognition may have a place, but the recognition that most of your staff and co-workers want is to hear a simple thank you from time to time.

At first, you may feel nervous and uncomfortable when recognizing others. This is natural, especially if recognition is new to you and your workplace. To overcome this awkwardness, begin with small steps. Pick a few simple techniques from this or another book on staff recognition that will work for you and your staff. With practice, you will become more comfortable letting others know that you appreciate what they do. You will grow your own repertoire of staff recognition techniques, which will make it easier for you to provide meaningful and **Appropriate** recognition.

"The problem today is that it's a rare company, and an exceptional leader, who dares to devote the time and make the effort to form the human relationship with co-workers that lead to the commitment and to the unleashing of human potential we all say we're looking for…We must make unleashing the potential of people a strategic imperative."
— Gary Heil, Tom Parker and Deborah C. Stephens, One Size Fits One

"Recognition is bad for morale. Others will resent my recognizing one of their co-workers."

This could be true, if the recognition is seen as undeserved or unfair. If one worker or a team is recognized frequently while the contributions and achievements of others are consistently ignored, others may be resentful. Justifiably so—it looks like favouritism.

It's not that everyone should receive an equal quantity of recognition. Some supervisors feel that treating everyone the same would be easier. It could be, but it would also be dishonest. Recognition should be based on performance. Top performers who see underachievers receiving the same recognition as they do may view this as unfair, which may cause them to consider leaving— either physically, or just by switching to cruise control.

If recognition is bestowed regularly on all staff for specific contributions and achievements, those not being recognized today will celebrate the success of their co-workers, knowing that their turn will come. They understand that good performance is appreciated and will be praised.

"No one ever recognized me and look how well I've done. I can't see why it needs to be different for the people who work for me."

Recognition—or the lack of it—isn't about you. It is about the people who you supervise and those with whom you work. Obviously, you were a good worker and self-motivated. It also appears that you were cheated out of the recognition you deserved. This was wrong, just as it would be wrong for you to withhold recognition from deserving individuals when they perform well. It is dangerous to assume that your staff is made up of people who are as self-motivated as you are. Some will be, but others will need your praise and encouragement to remain engaged and productive.

Before reading further, ask yourself these questions: What would have happened if you had received more positive feedback along the way? Would you have reached your potential sooner? Might you have achieved even more if your supervisors had expressed appreciation more often?

"Tenderness and kindness are not signs of weakness and despair, but manifestations of strength and resolution."
— Kahlil Gabran, poet & writer

"If I recognize them for doing something well, what happens when they don't do well? Won't they use the fact that I recognized them previously against me if I criticize their work?"
Recognizing people for doing their jobs well does not mean that they should not be corrected or reprimanded for failing to perform satisfactorily.

Part of a manager or supervisor's role is to provide both positive and negative feedback as required. They should reinforce good performances and confront and correct poor performances.

The best way to avoid having employees use previous positive comments to defend themselves from negative feedback is to ensure that all feedback is specific. Focus on a single action or event. Avoid generalizations about the individual's performance ("You always do a wonderful job," or "You never get anything right the first time.") Whether praising or reprimanding, it is important to focus on the person's actions and not his personality. Focus your feedback on the quality of the performance and not the quality of the person performing the task.

Generally, supervisors and managers seem better at—or at least, more focused on—noting what has gone poorly, rather than letting people know when they have done well. This is despite the fact that most staff members are dedicated, committed and doing their jobs well.

Not only would more positive feedback be the right thing to do, it may also reduce the need to provide as much negative feedback. Any type of meaningful feedback helps staff know what is expected of them. Positive feedback leads them to repeat these desirable behaviours for which they are recognized.

"We found that the most exciting environments, that treated people very well, are also tough as nails. There is no bureaucratic mumbo-jumbo... excellent companies provide two things simultaneously: tough environments and very supportive environments."
— Tom Peters, author

DIY RECOGNITION RESEARCH:
Making a List, Checking It Twice

What you will need for this research project:
Pen and paper

Research Process:
Divide the paper into three columns.

Employees/Co-workers	What this person did well	Recognized?
	1. 2. 3.	❑ ❑ ❑
	1. 2. 3.	❑ ❑ ❑
	1. 2. 3.	❑ ❑ ❑
	1. 2. 3.	❑ ❑ ❑
	1. 2. 3.	❑ ❑ ❑

1. In the first column, list the names of 5 employees or co-workers.
2. In the second column, write three things that each person has done well over the past month.
3. In the third column, put a check mark next to each of these well-done tasks for which you have recognized this person.
4. Count the number of check marks.

Implications for the Workplace:
• Score your responses

Number of Check Marks

13 – 15 Congratulations! You understand the importance of staff recognition and have been "walking the talk." You should write a book on staff recognition.

9 – 12 You're doing well. Sometimes we miss opportunities to recognize people for a job well done. Commit to being more alert for times when you can let staff know they are appreciated.

6 – 8 You're doing okay, but you will need to pay more attention to staff recognition. Try some of the ideas that you will find in this book.

5 or fewer You have a way to go, but you have taken an important first step by reading this book. Find a few ideas you feel comfortable with and begin with them.

Hint: Now that you have a list of reasons to recognize staff, go and do it!

Please note that this form is available online at:
www.GREATstaffrecognition.com/bookbonus/DIYforms
You have permission to print it for your use to conduct this recognition research.

SECTION ONE
The Road to Recognition Hell

Chapter 1
Paved with Good Intentions

People who create staff recognition programs are well-intentioned individuals. They understand that people are key to the organization's success and that most employees work hard. Staff deserve to be acknowledged for their contributions and successes—for what they do and what they achieve for the organization.

Unfortunately, recognition programs often lose their focus. What they were meant to recognize is replaced with whatever the person using the program wants to recognize, or feels should be recognized. Frequently, they become bogged down with rules. Unfocused and cumbersome, programs become ineffective staff recognition tools.

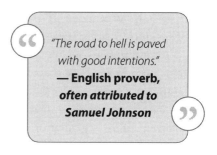

"The road to hell is paved with good intentions."
— **English proverb, often attributed to Samuel Johnson**

Today's supervisors were once the people being supervised. They recall what it was like. They remember how they felt when their contributions were acknowledged and their work was praised. Being recognized felt good.

They may also recall what it was like to be dumped on all the time, when all they ever heard from their supervisors was bad news. Back then, they vowed that things would be different when they became supervisors. They would treat those that they supervised better than they had been treated.

Most of today's supervisors preferred working for supervisors who acknowledged employees for their contributions. They understand that the same is true for the people they supervise. Their experience is consistent with what researchers have discovered. Meaningful staff recognition increases engagement and it is an effective staff-retention tool. People tend to stay where they feel valued.

The Challenge for Senior Executives

Elsewhere in the organization, there are senior executives who also understand the importance of staff recognition. They wish to express gratitude for what staff do, but are largely powerless to do anything about it. Superintendents of schools don't observe what happens in individual classrooms every day. Senior hospital administrators don't see what nurses, laboratory technicians or physical therapists do every shift. Corporate CEOs aren't in every branch office or store on a daily basis.

Their solution is to create corporate-wide recognition programs, hoping these will convey the message to staff that they are appreciated for their contributions. It would be more effective if executives encouraged informal recognition throughout the organization. They should begin by expressing appreciation for the contributions of managers and others who report directly to them, including acknowledging them for doing a good job of recognizing their staff. When executives leave their offices, they should also watch for behaviours by other staff that they are able to praise immediately.

In addition to people who initiate staff recognition programs for the right reasons, there are those whose motivation is less altruistic. They are not bestowing **Genuine** expressions of gratitude. *Appearing* to recognize staff is more important to them than actually recognizing staff. Their reasons are not **Relevant** to the organization's values, mission statement and goals.

Formal Recognition: *consists of a structured program with defined processes and criteria linked to organizational values and goals, a nomination and selection process, and an Awards ceremony where employees receive public recognition and are presented with awards in a formal setting. Generally speaking, it is an annual program and only a small percentage of employees are recognized.*
— Recognition Professionals International

Introducing a Staff Recognition Program
for All the Right—and Wrong—Reasons

The Right Reasons

- The managers and supervisors realize that staff are working hard and deserve to be acknowledged for that.
- The managers and supervisors feel that staff recognition is the right thing to do—staff deserve to be acknowledged for doing their jobs well.
- The managers and supervisors understand that most staff members want and need to be thanked for what they do.
- The managers and supervisors remember fondly when they worked for a boss who genuinely praised staff—and less fondly those whose approach to leadership was to demand and reprimand.
- The managers and supervisors know that research has shown that recognition is an effective staff retention tool—people stay where they know they are appreciated.

The Wrong Reasons

- The managers and supervisors want to improve satisfaction scores on staff attitude surveys.
- The managers and supervisors have been told by their superiors that they must recognize staff more.
- The managers and supervisors want to be able to demonstrate they are doing something to express appreciation to staff.
- The managers and supervisors want to control what happens related to staff recognition.
- The managers and supervisors feel that what is important about recognition are the tangibles—certificates, banquets, plaques and gifts—the bigger the better.
- The managers and supervisors want something that is seen as fair and politically correct. They believe that one staff recognition technique will fit all.
- The managers and supervisors are uncomfortable with spontaneous recognition; recognition is easier when provided according to a schedule.

So, What Is Being Recognized with Service Awards?

Service awards are the most common type of formal recognition. They are used to mark milestones in an employee's tenure with the organization, usually in multiples of five years, beginning on the employee's fifth anniversary. Frequently, the employee is presented with a pin or certificate to mark the occasion, along with a gift or gift card—the value of which varies, depending on the financial state of the organization and the length of service being recognized.

How the presentations are made varies. Some organizations invite the honoree and a guest to a recognition event, such as banquet or reception. Some fly those being honoured to another city, providing meals and accommodation in the hotel where the event is being held. Other times, presentations are made in the workplace, with only the honoree's co-workers present, or in the privacy of the supervisor's office. There are occasions when a pin, certificate or gift simply appears in the employee's mailbox one day, without any explanation or words of appreciation.

Putting a Value on Service

Organizations often have policies that assign a cash value to gifts presented to an employee who has reached specified service plateaus:

- $50 after 5 years of service
- $75 after 10 years of service
- $100 after 15 years of service
- $150 after 20 years of service

Imagine how employees might interpret the cash value associated with their years of service. After 10 years, an employee discovers his employer has assigned a value of $7.50 to each year he has worked for the company. That works out to less than four cents per work day. How special does that feel?

Having labelled service awards as an ineffective staff recognition tool, I must confess to having once created such a program, and must state my belief that there is nothing wrong with pausing to acknowledge those who have continued with the same employers for five, 10, 15 or more years. But let's be clear about what is being acknowledged. Often those presenting service awards—and occasionally those receiving them—seem confused about what is being recognized.

The CEO who stands before a banquet audience and proclaims that "these people are being recognized for all the great things they do for our company and our clients," just doesn't get it. Service awards are not about doing a great job. They recognize one, and one thing only:

Survival!

"We appreciate that you have remained with this organization. You have saved us the expense and task of hiring your replacement," might be a better message from the CEO.

Among any group of service-award recipients you will find quite a range of talent. There are top performers who deserve to be recognized for "doing great things." But there are others whose prime accomplishments over the past five years were to have done just enough to avoid being fired—and to have not died.

Long service is often equated with loyalty, but this isn't always the case. Some long-serving employees may not be so by choice. They have remained where they are because no other organization will make the same hiring error that you—or your predecessor, or the person before her—made five, 10, 15 or more years ago. Some long-serving employees are more disloyal than anyone who has left. They regularly bad-mouth their employer, shop in the competitors' stores, or sabotage (sometimes intentionally and sometimes inadvertently) efforts to achieve the company's goals. On the other hand, there are former employees who fondly recall working for the organization, and actively encourage others to apply for vacant positions.

Neither Pain or Fever Shall Keep Employees from Their Assigned Desks

Somewhere, sometime in the past, someone had this brilliant idea—combat absenteeism in a positive manner by rewarding those who showed up every day. Discourage poor behaviour (absenteeism) by rewarding good behaviour (attendance). The perfect attendance award was born.

Perfect-attendance awards seem to make sense. After all, absenteeism is seldom a good thing. When someone is away, productivity suffers. Tasks for which the absentee is responsible go undone. Projects are delayed. Co-workers become less productive because they require information or material that only their absent colleague can provide. They may be required to leave some aspect of their jobs undone to take up the slack.

Hiring replacement workers— if they are even available—can be expensive and they likely will be less productive than the people they are replacing. Customers become upset because the person with whom they have been dealing is unavailable.

Perfect-attendance awards work something like this: show up every day for a month or a year and we'll do something nice for you. Show up every day for twice as long and we'll do something nicer. Improve your attendance even more, and we will do something even nicer yet.

The underlying belief is that perfect attendance is desirable. This might be true, if the person who is present is healthy and productive. This employee's perfect attendance would certainly benefit the company, co-workers and customers. The only one who doesn't benefit is the potential replacement worker who doesn't have the opportunity to replace this employee—but there are likely lots of other opportunities to fill-in for someone else who is absent.

Assuming that the rewards of such a program are attractive to the employees, a perfect-attendance program is more likely to punish the person who may miss work occasionally for legitimate reasons than encourage chronically absent or late employees. No incentive will be significant enough to change the behaviour of those with attendance problems. Individual attendance problems should be addressed directly, with disciplinary action taken when necessary.

There are times when not being at work is better than maintaining a record of perfect attendance.

- Far better to spend a day or two at home wrapped in a blanket, drinking warm liquids and getting lots of rest, than dragging oneself into the office and trying to be productive, while running a fever of 39°C and sharing germs with co-workers and customers.
- Far better to spend an afternoon in the dentist's chair than trying to remain productive while suffering with an abscessed tooth.
- Far better to remain at home during the season's worst snowstorm than risking life and property just to get to work.

However, doing any of these sensible things will take the staff member out of the running for this year's perfect-attendance award. What attendance programs may do is encourage people who are sick to come to work, rather than stay in bed. The term for the resulting phenomenon is "presenteeism"—being physically present, but not functioning well.

A study by the Cornell University Institute for Health and Productivity suggests that sick people should stay away from work. In fact, they should be encouraged to stay away. Doing so can save employers money.

The researchers concluded that people who come to work sick with headaches, arthritis, asthma, allergies and mental health-related problems such as depression cost employers in lost productivity.

Sick people are less productive. They have trouble concentrating and take longer to complete tasks. They can also infect co-workers, which can lead to further productivity loss.

Productive or not, all employees who meet the basic criteria are rewarded for waking up on time and navigating their way to the office day after day over a specified time period. What they do after they punch-in doesn't matter. Perfect attendance programs reward people for where they are, not what they do.

One-in-a-hundred Chance of Being Recognized
Service and attendance awards do have a couple of things going for them:

- Both have criteria to determine eligibility for the awards—achieving a minimum number of years of service or days without an absence.
- Eventually everyone could qualify for the award.

The same cannot be said about most employee-of-the-month-type programs.

Anyone considering implementing an employee-of-the-month program should first do the math. There are only 12 months in a year. In an organization with 100 employees, each employee has only a one-in-a-hundred chance of being chosen each month. If everyone had a turn being the employee-of-the-month, it would take eight years and four months before the last person became the employee-of-the-month. This calculation assumes no turnover, which is unlikely if employees are only recognized once every eight years and four months.

The criteria for employee-of-the-month is often vague, such as going "above and beyond the call of duty." Not only is the meaning of "above and beyond" unclear, it can also become a moving target. Many factors, such as gender balance, length of service, improved performance and a desire to share the award among different job categories can influence who is selected as the employee-of-the-month.

Culture of Recognition

A culture of recognition can be illustrated with a series of concentric circles that form a model for meaningful staff recognition. At its core, recognition must be **Genuine**. Recognition fails when it is characterized by insincerity and empty rituals.

In the next circle there are four ingredients which, along with being **Genuine**, create the strong basis for meaningful staff recognition.

The next circle contains the tools and practices of informal, day-to-day recognition—the high-value, low-cost recognition that can be provided by supervisors and co-workers. This is the area in the model that, if filled with frequent and varied recognition, creates a foundation for formal recognition activities to be effective. The greater the amount of informal, day-to-day recognition, the greater the potential for formal recognition to be meaningful, although the demand for formal recognition is diminished.

Recognition fails when programs are dragged into the centre of the model, replacing the five basic ingredients of **GREAT** staff recognition—**Genuine, Relevant, Explicit, Appropriate** and **Timely.** A discussion of these five concepts begins in the next section of this book.

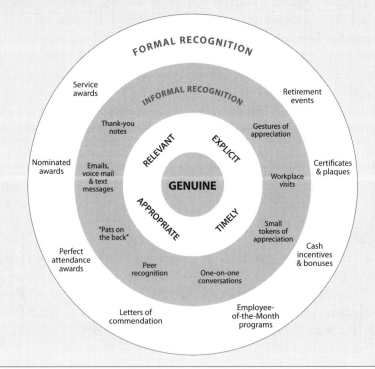

Where there is uncertainty about how the recipient will be selected from one month to the next, the award appears to be a popularity contest. Becoming employee-of-the-month is irrelevant to most and a joke to many. An employee-of-the-month program is ineffective as a means of expressing gratitude, despite the good intentions of those who introduced it.

> *"Nothing is more destructive of human dignity than a rule, which imposes a mute and blind obedience."*
> **— Anthony Eden, former British Prime Minister**

As part of my research, I have sought out current and previous employees-of-the-month. Most were shy to talk about the designation. They were unsure why they were selected over others, concluding on many occasions that it must just have been their turn. Others, who had never been the employee-of-the-month, could describe the process used to select the winners ("It's done by management from among people nominated by customers"), but were unsure about the criteria upon which the decision was based.

Programs Generate Rules

Programs may not generate feelings of being appreciated, but they always seem to create the need for policies. For every program, there seems to be an ever-expanding list of rules to which adherence seems more important than celebrating the accomplishments of staff.

> *"Common sense is the knack of seeing things as they are, and doing things as they ought to be done."*
> **— C.E. Stowe, *American author***

While they may not always begin that way, most programs are soon burdened by a myriad of rules—some of which may be real, many of which are imagined or made up on the fly, and most of which frustrate efforts to recognize staff:

- Once you have been the employee-of-the-month, you can't be the employee-of-the-month until everyone has had a turn. If being the employee-of-the-month was meant to motivate people, what motivation would exist when one realized that the next such recognition was likely years away?
- Employee-of-the-month recipients must come from different departments and reflect gender balance.
- Certain levels and types of absenteeism are acceptable and do not disqualify you from getting a perfect-attendance award (e.g., you are allowed to be absent for one day per quarter, but this is not cumulative; you may attend the funeral of a family member, but not a friend; you may attend dental or medical appointments that take less than two hours).
- An elaborative appeal process is in place for employees who believe they have been denied a service award for which they have qualified.
- One health-care facility with a high number of part-time employees calculates years of service based on hours worked, rather than calendar years. A half-time person will take 10 years to qualify for a five-year service award. (What about overtime? Is it credited at 1.5 time regular time? Looks like an opportunity to create another rule.)
- Perfect attendance is based on a rolling 12-month year. When a staff member returns after missing a day due to illness or a family crisis, the 12-month clock restarts at zero.

"You are remembered for the rules you break."
— Douglas MacArthur, *American general*

Without a Foundation, the Playhouse Collapsed

Back when our kids were young, I decided to build them a backyard playhouse. I didn't know anything about building a playhouse, but I had a design in mind. I envisioned an A-frame, with a door at one end and a window at the other. On one side, a ladder would lead up to a second floor, and on the other, a deck above the sandbox. A beam would extend out from the peak of the roof to which I would attach a rope on which the kids could swing. It would be perfect for our kids.

A weekend was set aside for this project. A work colleague–who knew as much about construction as I did–volunteered to assist me. Early that Saturday morning, I was off to the building-supply store to purchase everything I felt I would need—lumber, nails and an assortment of tools.

When Dave arrived, we set to work. Soon the frame of the playhouse took shape. Satisfied with our work to this stage, we retreated into the house for what we felt was a well-deserved break from our labours–and to reward ourselves with an essential ingredient to our success that I had picked up on the way home from the building supply store–beer.

We had just opened a couple of cans when there was a knock at the back door. It was Jamie, the boy who had been watching our construction project from across the alley.

"Mr. Scott, your playhouse just fell down."

Dave and I rushed to the kitchen window. Yes indeed, where the frame of the playhouse stood just minutes before, there was now a jumbled mass of two-by-fours. We would have to start over…but not before we had finished our beers, and maybe a couple more.

A few minutes later, there was another knock at the door. Jamie was back. And this time, he had his father–an engineer–in tow.

We joined them in the backyard, where the father surveyed our unsuccessful construction project. He explained that our efforts had failed because we had tried to erect the playhouse without first having a foundation upon which to build.

He suggested that we begin with six-by-six timbers, arranging them as a foundation for our project. Once this was done, we would have a base upon which to build a playhouse that wouldn't fall over.

We followed his advice, and eventually had a structure that would provide our children with years of play value. When we moved 24 years later, the playhouse–a little worse- for-wear and now used as a storage shed–was still standing. Without the solid foundation that Jamie's father had suggested, this would not have been possible.

Recognition programs–such as employee-of-the-month, and service and perfect- attendance awards–are like that playhouse. They are destined to collapse without a strong foundation. The playhouse needed a base of six-by-six timbers. Recognition programs need the foundation of a strong culture of appreciation, rooted in informal, day-to-day recognition that is meaningful to recipients and valued by staff.

Where Programs Would Be Most Meaningful, There Is Less Demand

If expressing gratitude is not part of the culture, formal recognition programs have little chance of success. Programs alone, installed in a work environment where informal recognition is rare, will not lead to greater engagement, better motivation or enhanced staff morale. High-value, low-cost staff recognition can.

Frequent and varied informal recognition creates a sound foundation for formal programs. The more informal recognition, the greater the potential for formal recognition programs to be meaningful to the staff.

Ironically, the more that informal recognition occurs, the less pressure executives and managers will feel to introduce formal recognition in response to staff members' expressions that they feel unappreciated.

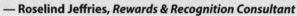

"Employees will be more receptive to formal, organization-wide programs if they believe that the company really cares about them on a personal, day-to-day basis."
— **Roselind Jeffries, *Rewards & Recognition Consultant***

Don't Cancel Your Recognition Program…Just Yet

If you are reading this book, you likely fall into one of two groups. You have one or more recognition programs in place, but feel they aren't delivering a good return on your investment. Or nothing much is happening in your organization to let staff know that their efforts are appreciated and you are searching for strategies to introduce more recognition into your workplace. Maybe you are thinking about creating a staff recognition program.

If you have a staff recognition program, I am not going to tell you to discard it. But I won't be disappointed to hear that after examining the effectiveness of your program you decide to phase it out. Are the benefits your organization receive justifying the investment of time, money and other resources that it takes?

If you don't have a program, I suggest that you not start one. It would be foolishly optimistic to believe that a recognition program or two would create a culture of recognition in your workplace. Focus on introducing more informal, day-to-day recognition—high-value, low-cost staff recognition.

"[The] primary focus of effective recognition efforts is on creating a true culture of recognition, not launching programs or hosting events."
— Bob Nelson, *"The Importance of Strategic Recognition"*
Human Resource Executive

DIY RECOGNITION RESEARCH:
You Are the Employee-of-the-Month Because...?

What you need to conduct this research:
An organization that displays photos or names of its current and former employees-of-the-month, the chutzpah to ask a few questions.

Research Process:
1. Seek out the employee-of-the-month. Ask, "Why were you selected as the employee-of-the-month?"
2. Listen to the response. Note particularly responses such as, "I dunno" or "I guess it was my turn."
3. Next, seek out previous employees-of-the-month (if they still work there). Ask, "Why were you only the employee-of-the-month once? Haven't you been doing a good job since?"
4. Listen to the responses. Note particularly responses such as, "You can only be the employee-of-the-month once," or "Everyone has to have a turn to be the employee-of-the-month."
5. Be prepared to leave quietly when asked to do so by store security.

Supplementary Questions (for added credit):
- "When you were selected as the employee-of-the-month, was it because you were the most productive employee, or just because it was your turn?"
- "How did being selected as the employee-of-the-month change how you regard your company and supervisor? Did it make you feel more appreciated for what you do?"

Implications for the Workplace:
Do your staff members know why they are recognized? Do they feel recognition comes because they have done a good job, or do they simply feel people are recognized because it's their turn?

Hint: If recipients don't know why they are being recognized, there is a need to link recognition to what the organization says is important—its mission statement, values and goals.

G enuine
R elevant
E xplicit
A ppropriate
T imely

SECTION TWO
GREAT Staff Recognition

Chapter 2
The 5 Ingredients That Make
Staff Recognition GREAT

I think I have always had a special relationship with the number five. I don't know when it began, or why. But five has been my favourite number for as long as I can remember. Maybe it's just about having five fingers on each hand or five toes on each foot.

In school, I learned to count by fives. And the five-times table was the easiest part of learning the multiplication facts. If I did something well, the teacher would attach a sticker to my assignment—one that was star-shaped with five points.

When I was a kid, five cents was actually worth something. There were five-cent chocolate bars and five-cent ice-cream cones. It only took five cents to mail a letter to Grandma.

My first "job" was as a newspaper carrier, and what did I charge my customers for their daily newspaper? Five cents. When was 12, I had an article published in our local weekly newspaper. It was the first money I ever earned for something I wrote. The editor paid me the princely sum of five cents per column inch when it appeared in his newspaper.

About the same time, I began listening to jazz on the radio. The Dave Brubeck Quartet was getting a lot of radio time with its newly-released *Take Five,* written by band member Paul Desmond. Eventually, that single reached No. 5 on *Billboard's* Adult Contemporary chart.

In the world of work, five seems to have some significance, as well. Five defines the length of the typical work week. After five years, companies begin to give employees service awards and continue to do so, every five years thereafter.

And five minutes is enough time to write a thank-you note, to compose a congratulatory email, or to leave your office to acknowledge an employee for a contribution and return—or stay to discover another example of a job well done.

"There are only five notes in the musical scale, but their variations are so many that they cannot all be heard. There are only five basic colours, but their variations are so many that they cannot all be seen. There are only five basic flavours, but their variations are so many that they cannot all be tasted.
— Sun Tzu, *The Art of War*

Great Performances by Great Staff Deserve GREAT Recognition.

And most importantly for me, recognition that is most meaningful and valued by recipients has five ingredients that are represented in the five-letter acronym **GREAT**:

Genuine
Relevant
Explicit
Appropriate
Timely

These are the building blocks of staff recognition. Not all five pieces need to be present in every statement of appreciation for it to be meaningful, but *one* is essential to any expression of gratitude. Staff recognition must always be **Genuine.**

The person expressing appreciation must *genuinely* believe—and the recipient must know—that recognition is deserved. Recognition that is insincere, given because it is the "thing to do," or offered to an undeserving recipient is meaningless and diminishes the credibility of future recognition.

"Good praise is timely, sincere and specific. It focuses solely on the positive and is best when personally delivered."
— Bob Nelson, *author*

Once you begin with **Genuine** belief that recognition is warranted, you need to add at least one of the other ingredients to express gratitude. The more ingredients you add, the stronger the message of appreciation becomes.

Recognition that is **Relevant** relates to what the organization says is important, often expressed in the form of a vision, mission statement, values or goals. **Relevant** recognition focuses on behaviours that are key to employees' on-the-job success, be it as part of the team and as an individual.

Explicit recognition makes the reason for recognition clear. There is a specific description of what the recipient did that is deserving of recognition.

Appropriate is about knowing staff members as individuals—their strengths, their passions, their interests—and, of course, their recognition preferences. **Appropriate** is understanding that not every member fits into the same square or round staff recognition hole—there are some whose recognition preferences are shaped more like an oval, triangle or octagon.

Recognition does not improve with age. The longer you wait to recognize someone, the less its impact. **Timely** recognition is delivered within hours or days of the event for which the recipient is being acknowledged, not weeks or months later.

Each of the next five chapters focuses on a different element of **GREAT** staff recognition. They include more in-depth discussion of the ingredients, stories that illustrate why they are important, and practical suggestions to deliver **GREAT** staff recognition, that is **Genuine, Relevant, Explicit, Appropriate** and **Timely.**

"Praise is a gift gently wrapped in thoughtful words and gracious gestures carefully chosen with the recipient in mind."
— Sharon F. Marks, *It Pays to Praise*

Chapter 3
The Wisdom of Baby Bear

Baby Bear was excited. In his paw he held something that almost made him forget what had happened a few days earlier. That was the day when he came home to discover his little bowl empty, his favourite chair in pieces and a girl asleep on his bed.

Today, things were pretty much back to normal in the Three Bears' home. Mama Bear cooked porridge and ladled it into three bowls on the dining room table—a big bowl for Papa Bear, a middle-sized bowl for Mama Bear and a little bowl for Baby Bear. While the porridge cooled, the Three Bears went for a walk.

In the only departure from past practice, Papa Bear now checked to ensure the doors were locked and all the windows were latched before leaving the house. The Three Bears didn't want a repeat of the Goldilocks incident.

On that morning, Baby Bear had cried out, "Someone has been sleeping in my bed and she's still there!" His shrieks had awakened the little girl. With three puzzled, furry creatures peering down at her, Goldilocks leapt from the bed, bounded down the stairs and out the front door. She hadn't stopped running until she was out of the woods. Safely back inside her house, Goldilocks had sat down at her writing desk.

When the Three Bears returned from today's morning walk, Mama found three envelopes in the mailbox. One was addressed to Papa Bear. One was addressed to Mama Bear. And one was addressed to Baby Bear.

Mama Bear handed an envelope to Baby Bear. "It's from Goldilocks," she said.

"Open it," Papa Bear said. "What does that little girl have to say for herself?"

Baby Bear tore open the envelope and removed a card decorated with little pink flowers. He began to read:

> *Dear Baby Bear –*
>
> *How are you? I am fine. I really enjoyed visiting your home recently. I had such a great time. Thank you for everything. I appreciated your hospitality. I wish I could have stayed longer so we could have gotten to know each other better.*
>
> *Have a good day!*
>
> *Your friend,*
> *Goldilocks*

"Isn't that nice?" Mama Bear said.

"She is such a thoughtful girl," Papa Bear said.

Baby Bear said nothing, but his smile extended from ear to ear.

Mama Bear picked up her envelope and studied the return address. "My letter is also from Goldilocks." She opened the envelope, removed a card decorated with little pink flowers, and began to read aloud:

> *Dear Mama Bear –*
>
> *How are you? I am fine. I really enjoyed visiting your home recently. I had such a great time. Thank you for everything. I appreciated your hospitality. I wish I could have stayed longer so we could have gotten to know each other better.*
>
> *Have a good day!*
>
> *Your friend,*
> *Goldilocks*

40

"Isn't that nice?" Mama Bear said, as she laid the note next to her bowl of porridge.

"She is such a thoughtful girl," Papa Bear said.

Baby Bear still said nothing, but that huge grin was beginning to fade.

Now it was Papa Bear's turn to read from a card decorated with little pink flowers:

Dear Papa Bear –

How are you? I am fine. I really enjoyed visiting your home recently. I had such a great time. Thank you for everything. I appreciated your hospitality. I wish I could have stayed longer so we could have gotten to know each other better.

Have a good day!

Your friend,
Goldilocks

Before Mama Bear had finished uttering, "Isn't that nice?" Baby Bear had crumpled his thank-you note and slammed it down so hard that his porridge spilled and began to drip onto the floor.

"It's not nice at all!" he screamed. "And she's not thoughtful either!"

His eyes filled with tears, Baby Bear ran from the table, past his now-repaired little chair, up the stairs and into his bedroom. He threw himself onto his little bed. His confused parents followed him up the stairs.

"What's wrong, Baby Bear?" Papa Bear asked.

"Why are you so upset, Baby Bear?" Mama Bear asked. "Why are you crying?"

"When Goldilocks came to our house, she tasted your porridge, but she didn't eat it all up," said Baby Bear, between sobs. "She sat in your chairs, but she didn't break them into pieces. And she lay down on your beds, but she didn't go to sleep on them."

"But, when she got home, she wrote such nice thank-you notes to each of us," Mama Bear said.

Baby Bear stopped crying long enough to wail: "She wrote the *same* thank-you note to each of us!"

"Yes, they did say the same thing, but each of us got our own card, with our names on them," Papa Bear responded.

"That was the only difference," Baby Bear said. "She didn't say anything about eating all of my porridge or breaking my chair or sleeping in my bed. I don't think that she really cares. She only wrote the thank-you notes because someone else told her she should do it.

"And," he added, 'I hate little pink flowers! I'm 'lergic to them.'"

Then Baby Bear said something that captured the essence of his anger. "It wasn't **Genuine**. She didn't really mean any of it!"

Baby Bear was right. Despite their daughter's predilection towards break and entry, vandalism and petty theft, Goldilocks' parents had taught her all the social niceties. Good manners had been emphasized. She had been drilled in proper etiquette, including how to follow up social

"When the spirit does not work with the hand, there is no art."
— Leonardo da Vinci

visits. She knew she should thank people for their hospitality. So as soon as she had returned from her harrowing adventure in the woods, she had sat down to write a thank-you note to each member of the Bear family in her very best handwriting. She always did what she had always been told she should always do.

In this, Goldilocks had something in common with some of today's managers and supervisors. For her, writing thank-you notes was a ritual. For them, recognition is a ritual.

This type of recognition doesn't work. Employees know that they and their co-workers contribute in different ways, at difference performance levels, and with different degrees of commitment. When they learn that they all received the same message of appreciation, they soon doubt the sincerity of the message and its author.

Goldilocks-type recognizers understand that it is important to express appreciation for how staff contributes and what they achieve. They have seen the research that says recognition can increase staff motivation and commitment, and improve retention. They may have read books—such as this one—that are filled with tips and techniques. They are equipped to go through the motions of staff recognition, but seem to have no emotional connection to the process.

A supervisor for whom recognition is an intellectual exercise knows when to recognize in a classic stimulus-response sort of way. Specific actions trigger specific recognition: completion of a project, an employee reaching a service anniversary or the arrival of a designated day or week. Each results in a predictable (a.k.a. ritualized) recognition response. Always. Every time. In the same fashion. These gestures sound as hollow as they are.

These supervisors seek programs and trinkets to express appreciation for them, rather than using simple day-to-day gestures that have high value to the recipients. They are always careful to recognize everyone equally for fear that someone will feel left out and unfairly treated. By doing so, they run the greater risk of alienating top performers and reinforcing below-average work.

Staff understand what's going on. They are quick to sniff out insincere praise and recognition. Just like Baby Bear, they know when someone is just going through the motions, providing recognition because "it is the thing to do." Or because senior managers have decreed that supervisors must recognize staff more often. Employees know this type of recognition isn't **Genuine**.

> "Anything you buy by the gross probably won't be reinforcing for very long."
> — **Janis Allen,**
> ***I Saw What You Did & I Know Who You Are: Giving and Receiving Recognition***

Such recognition can be worse than no recognition at all. The individual being recognized feels that the person providing the recognition doesn't know him, doesn't care about him and doesn't understand what he does. When everyone is thanked in the same way, it suggests that supervisors are not paying attention to what individuals do.

Telling someone he did a great job, when everyone knows he didn't, reduces the supervisor's credibility and damages her ability to deliver **Genuine** recognition when it is deserved.

The "Genuine" Recognizer

Recognition is truly meaningful only when the person providing recognition feels the need to recognize at an emotional level. **Genuine** recognition comes from the heart.

Genuine recognition is seen, heard and felt as being honestly deserved and honestly delivered. **Genuine** recognition thrives in a climate of mutual respect and trust. Supervisors who respect and trust employees for who they are and what they do, in turn receive respect and trust from their staff.

Note the sequencing of that last sentence. "Supervisors who respect and trust employees for who they are and what they do, in turn receive respect and trust from their staff." The order is important. It is a lesson that I learned from high school students.

For a number of years, our consulting company conducted annual student attitude surveys for a school district. One question asked students to, "Think of one staff member who has made a difference in your school career. What made that person special?" Year after year, students in one high school explained why a particular teacher had their respect. Most noteworthy about their descriptions was how they felt this teacher had earned their respect by first showing respect for them.

Like some managers and supervisors, there are teachers who believe that they are owed respect from their students by virtue of their positions. Others, such as that high school teacher, understand that respect does not come with the territory. Respect is earned. The most effective way for teachers to earn respect is to show respect for their students first. This is a lesson that transfers well from the classroom to the world of work. Employees are more likely to respond with respect when treated with respect.

In workplaces where **Genuine** recognition thrives, staff members feel valued for who they are and what they do. These workers are more energized, more engaged and more committed to their work, the company, their supervisors and their co-workers. Companies with reputations for providing **Genuine** recognition have less trouble attracting qualified applicants—and with lower turnover, have to fill positions less often.

Genuine recognition does not come from programs, but from people: supervisors and co-workers who consistently watch for opportunities to recognize others and take advantage of those opportunities when they arise.

"What comes from the heart, goes to the heart."
— **Samuel Taylor Coleridge,**
British poet

At Least 12 Clues that Employees Use to Identify When Recognition is More Ritual than Genuine:

1. The message is generic. Everyone hears the same words or receives the same letter of commendation.
2. Recognition seems to depend on tokens of appreciation—baseball caps, company jackets, certificates, plaques or bonuses.
3. Recognition is impersonal. Recognition usually occurs in groups, rather than individually. The focus is on events, rather than day-to-day recognition. Gifts are sent, not presented in person.
4. Recognition isn't spontaneous. It is saved until the next scheduled event.
5. The person making the presentation doesn't know the person being recognized, can't pronounce his name, doesn't know what he did or understand why it was important.
6. The recognition is calendar-specific, happening only on specific dates (birthdays, employment anniversaries, employee recognition days) or during special weeks (Administrative Professionals Week, Education Week, Nurses Week, etc.).
7. The person doing the recognition lays it on too thick, as if he hopes that among many platitudes there will be at least one that fits the circumstance.
8. Someone who the employee doesn't respect or doesn't trust delivers the recognition.
9. The recognition is disproportionate to what was achieved, such as presenting someone who just saved a million dollars with the same mug as everyone gets, or calling everyone together to celebrate someone completing a simple, routine task on time.
10. Recognition is used to buffer bad news. The only time an employee is praised is just before he is told what he did wrong.
11. The words of praise are out of sync with the tone of voice or body language of the recognizer.
12. There appears to be no relationship between the words of appreciation and anything the recipient did.

 "Some fellows pay a compliment like they expected a receipt."
— Kin Hubbard

At Least 15 Ways to Ensure
that Recognition is Genuine

1. Really care about the people with whom you work and about what they do.

2. Create an environment of trust and respect. Relationships between supervisors and employees are important in creating a culture where **Genuine** recognition thrives.

3. Search for reasons to recognize others. Once you start looking for reasons, you will find them.

4. Express your emotions. Let the recipient know how you feel about his actions—this shows the individual nature of your praise.

5. Be consistent. Recognize what deserves to be recognized, no matter who did it, when or where. And never recognize what doesn't warrant recognition, just because you feel bad that Joe has not been recognized recently. Wait and watch. His turn will come.

6. When recognizing staff, make eye contact and use the person's name. Eye contact conveys your sincerity. Using names, especially the person's first name, makes the process seem friendlier.

7. Focus on informal, day-to-day recognition rather than formal recognition. Use thank-you cards, rather than letterhead. Recognize in private, rather than always in public. Your purpose is to recognize others for doing a good job; not to demonstrate to others what a good job you do of recognizing staff.

8. Remember: how you say something is more important than the words you use. Speak from the heart, not a script. Feelings are more important than well-crafted words. Heartfelt recognition is always worth doing.

9. Before recognizing someone, turn off your cell phone. That's right. Turn it off; don't just switch it to vibrate. That way you won't be interrupted mid-acknowledgement. You won't have to decide who's more important, the person who you are recognizing or the person on the phone. Actually, it's really a no-brainer. The person being recognized is always more important. The caller can leave a message, because now is the time to express gratitude for a job well done. You can always return your boss's call when you're done.

10. In formal recognition situations, ensure that recognition comes from the right person—the most senior official who has some personal knowledge of the person being recognized and what she does.

11. Keep it short and simple. The longer and more flowery a presentation, the more artificial it seems.

12. Frame certificates when you give them to staff. This shows that you believe they are important and that the recipients should as well.

13. Provide honest feedback. When someone screws up, tell him. When he succeeds, tell him. Both types of feedback will be more believable.

14. Be **Explicit.** Focus recognition on specific performance and achievements of individuals and work groups. The more focused the recognition, the more **Genuine** it seems. Generic phrases sound disingenuous.

15. Say what you mean and mean what you say. There is no need to embellish. Explain how the person's action was **Relevant** to the company's purpose and how it helped the company achieve its goals.

"Flattery is from the teeth out. Sincere appreciation is from the heart out."
— **Dale Carnegie, *American writer***

G enuine
R elevant
E xplicit
A ppropriate
T imely

Chapter 4
Mission Misunderstood = Mission Impossible

How does your organization judge its success? More to the point, how do your customers judge your success?

For customers, it's not just about products and services. It is also about the *promises* that are implicit in your mission and value statements. Are you delivering as promised?

Your success depends on your employees, most of whom want to know what is expected of them to be successful in their jobs. Having employees who know what is expected of them at work was identified by The Gallup Organization as one of the 12 elements of great managing. "Groups that have high scores on this item were more productive, more profitable, and even more creative. Substantial gains on the first element alone often correlate with productivity gains of five to 10 per cent, thousands more happy customers and 10- to 20-per cent fewer on-the-job accidents."

One might think that the answer to the question, "What is expected of me at work?" would naturally flow from the organization's mission statement and goals, but this is often not the case. Front-line staff seem unaware of what leadership believes is key to the organization's success.

Visitors to America's gambling and entertainment capital are assured that, "What happens in Vegas stays in Vegas." A similar warning might be applied to mission statements and goal setting: "What happens in strategic planning sessions stays in the executive offices."

Organizations can spend a great deal of time discussing their purpose, defining their beliefs, and determining what they wish to achieve. Strategic planning sessions lead to vision and mission statements, values and goals. The foundation statements that come from these planning events are carefully worded, framed and hung on walls throughout the organization. There are presentations made by senior executives, complete with PowerPoint slides, and articles that appear in internal publications.

And then, nothing!

The planning and hype done, everyone gets back to doing what they would have done anyway. Occasionally, employees may glance towards a framed copy of the company's mission statement and values, and wonder to themselves, "What has that got to do with my job?" People don't see how these values apply to their daily work lives.

 "If your organization has taken the time and effort to clearly establish a core mission, values and strategies, then your reward and recognition systems should clearly and systematically reward the behaviors and outputs that reinforce those elements."
— **Bob Nelson, *"The Importance of Strategic Recognition,"* Human Resource Executive**

Recognition as a Communications Tool

Getting people to act in ways that reflect what the organization feels is important is a matter of communication. Certainly, this involves the posting of framed copies of the mission statement and values throughout the organization, presentations by senior executives, and articles in internal publications.

These communication activities only help create awareness. More is needed to ensure understanding and commitment.

Staff recognition is an under-utilized communication tool to translate the generalizations of mission statements and values into concrete, on-the-ground, day-to-day actions by front-line staff. **Relevant** staff recognition is aligned with what the organization says is important. **Relevant** recognition enhances understanding of the mission statement and values.

The organization's guiding principles will become meaningful only when they become **Relevant** to every employee's daily work life. This isn't going to happen because well-crafted, impressive-sounding words appear on the wall. It won't happen because of articles in staff newsletters, postings on the web-

Saying One Thing,
But Recognizing Another

Organizations often say that one thing is important, but appear to value something quite different:

What is said	What is recognized:
"We want employees to maintain a healthy work/life balance."	Working long hours, evenings and weekends
"Wellness is important. Employees should take care of their health and well-being. Sick time is there to be taken by those who are not felling well."	Perfect attendance
"Innovation and risk-taking are key to our success."	Following the book. Doing things according to policy and rules, the way we have always done things. Rather than being applauded for their initiative, those who take risks and fail are punished.
"Teamwork is key to our success."	Individual achievements
"Teaching undergrad students is this university's priority."	Research and publishing articles in academic journals
"Everyone has a role in mentoring new staff."	Getting one's own work done.
"We want to build long-term relationships with customers."	Quarterly sales results.

 "Having a vision is very important because if you don't know where you are going, you are already there."
— Unknown

site, PowerPoint presentations, or speeches by senior executives.

"Mission statements, synergies, strategies, visions— they are often ambiguous to the point of being meaningless."
— Chip Heath & Dan Heath, *Made to Stick*

Employees won't believe what is written until they see these values reflected in their supervisors' and managers' actions. Employees notice what you notice. They notice what you talk about. If your actions and talk reflect what your mission statement and values say are important, staff will notice them. When staff is recognized for behaviours that move the organization closer to its goals, those being recognized will understand and others will notice.

Relevant recognition makes the abstract real. Celebrating the right contributions by employees reinforces what the organization says is important. Knowing that behaviours which align with the mission statement, values and goals are valued focuses employees on these guiding principles.

Any time a supervisor recognizes a staff member for a job well done is a good time to talk about the mission, value statements and goals. **Relevant** recognition creates emotional connections between the recipient and those who witness the recognition, and the organization's goals and values.

Shining Light on What's Important

This is not always easy to do. While important, **Relevant** behaviours are not always the easiest to observe and quantify. Recognition is frequently focused on what is easy to see—perfect attendance, years of service, a work area free of clutter. The actions that have the greatest potential for real, long-term and sustained impact often pass unnoticed and unacknowledged.

Think about the couple who were passing a darkened parking lot one evening when they noticed a man on his hands and knees, frantically searching for something under a street lamp. They approached and asked if they could help.

"I dropped my keys and can't find them," the man said.

The couple joined the search. After a few minutes the woman asked, "Where were you when you lost your keys?"

"Over there," he responded, pointed to a dark corner of the parking lot.

"If you lost them over there, why are you looking for them here?" the husband asked.

" 'Cuz the light's better here."

No matter how long he searched, this man was going to be unsuccessful.

Good lighting was irrelevant to his success. In the same way, recognizing staff for behaviours unrelated to the organization's goals is not going to contribute to it meeting those goals. Recognition is most effective when it is focused on what's needed for the organization to succeed and the on-the-job success of individual employees. Behaviours that drive business results should be the behaviours for which people are recognized.

Ask Staff, "What's Needed to Succeed?"

In addition to looking at what the organization's foundation documents say, it is important to ask employees—the ones who know their job best—what behaviours are key to their on-the-job success.

While staff members may be asked for input during group meetings, it can be more informative to meet with each person whose work you supervise, to talk about their work and how they feel they contribute to the company meeting its goals. Every meeting could be an opportunity to learn how each worker views his job and clear up misconceptions about the work and the direction the company is going. Questions such as these could be used to guide the conversations:

- Tell me about your job? What do you do? How do you do this? What makes this the best way to do your job?
- What do you need to do to be successful on the job?
- How do you feel your work contributes to the success of your co-workers, our department and the entire organization?
- Describe a recent task that you completed successfully. What did you need to do to be successful?
- What are you being asked to do that is inconsistent with the organization's mission and value statements, or our stated goals?
- What gets in the way of you getting things done? What could be changed to increase your success or to enable you to contribute more to the department and the organization?

In what you hear, you will discover what the people doing the work feel is relevant to their success and for what they should be recognized. When employees know that supervisors understand what they need to do to succeed, they will value the recognition they receive.

At Least 14 Ways to Keep Recognition Relevant

1. Encourage staff to set job targets that are consistent with the organization's mission and value statements, and goals. Recognize them for making progress and for achieving the goals they set for themselves.

2. When recognizing staff for doing their jobs well, highlight how their actions have assisted the organization in meeting its goals. Emphasize how a teacher's behaviour contributed to student learning, or how the way things are done in a warehouse results in orders being filled quickly and customers waiting less time for shipments.

3. Review your mission and value statements. List behaviours that will move your organization closer to these desired outcomes. When you witness these behaviours, acknowledge and thank the employee. Visit www. GREATstaffrecognition.com/bookbonus/behaviours for examples of behaviours that reflect a few of the values that organizations commonly set for themselves.

4. Let staff know what behaviours you expect. Make a list. Talk about it. Publish it. Post it on bulletin boards. Praise people when you see these behaviours.

5. Don't just tell employees. Ask them what your values mean. Invite them to suggest ways to meet your goals of reducing costs, providing exceptional customer service, improving quality, or becoming more environmentally conscious. Tell them what you are going to do with their suggestions. Which ones are you going to use? Or not use? Explain why. Give credit to those whose suggestions you use.

6. Recognize both outcomes (meeting pre-defined goals, completing a project on time, etc.) and behaviour (listening to a patient's concerns, keeping filing up-to-date, etc.)

7. Reread your mission and value statements. Are they full of concepts like risk-taking, innovation, honesty, exceeding customers' expectations, teamwork, learning, etc.? Are employees recognized—or punished—for demonstrating these traits?

 "If you've got really smart people who are all focused on the same mission, then usually you can get some things done."
— President Barack Obama

8. List the values that are important to your company. Identify behaviours that are characteristic of these values. Now list employees who demonstrate these behaviours. If you aren't already doing it, let them know you appreciate what they do to support the company's values. Then, continue to recognize them for doing so.

9. Select one of your organization's values (teamwork, customer service, innovation) as the staff recognition focus for the week. Watch for examples of behaviours that reflect that value. When you see it, speak to the person. Describe what you saw, explain why it is important and express your appreciation.

10. Order mouse pads with your mission statement, values and goals printed on them. Staff will be reminded of these every time they use their computers.

11. Listen carefully when customers praise a staff member's actions. They are telling you what is important to them and why they continue to do business with you. Are these the same behaviours for which you recognize your staff?

12. When customers complain about a staff member's actions, they are telling you what they don't want. Be sure these are not the behaviours for which staff is recognized.

13. Match consequences (recognition) to desired behaviour:
    - When creating schedules for the next work period, offer those with the best attendance and on-time work records the first choice of when to work.
    - Recognize those who show up on time for staff meetings by entering their names in a draw for an extended coffee or lunch break.
    - When selecting a gift to acknowledge someone for his promotion, find something he can use in his new job.

14. Tell stories about employees who have performed in ways that contribute to the organization's success. Like all good stories, your tales of success should conclude with a moral—one that reflects the organization's mission statement, values or goals (See Chapter 27, "Doing Recognition Right," for more on making storytelling part of how you recognize staff).

 "The first responsibility of a leader is to define reality. The last is to say thank you. In between, the leader is a servant."
— Max DePree, Leadership is an Art

 **DIY RECOGNITION RESEARCH:**
Are the Right Behaviours Being Recognized?

What you will need to conduct this research:
A chart similar to the one below, a copy of your organization's mission statement, values and goals.

Research Procedure:
1. Complete Column 1 of the chart below by listing behaviours for which you or others have recognized staff recently.
2. Complete Column 2 by matching each behaviour to your mission statement or one of your values or goals.

Column 1	Column 2
List five reasons for which you have seen staff recognized recently (by you or others)	To which mission, value, or goal statement does each of these behaviours relate?
1.	
2.	
3.	
4.	
5.	

Workplace Implications:
Scoring
4 – 5 matches: Congratulations! The recognition staff is receiving is **Relevant** to what the organization says is important.
2 – 3 matches: Pretty good! The recognition staff is receiving is generally **Relevant** to what the organization says is important, but there is room for improvement to strengthen messages of appreciation.
0 – 1 matches: Not good, but likely typical of the level of relevance of recognition that occurs in most organizations. Improvement is possible.

Hint: Recognition that is aligned to your values and goals becomes a regular reminder of what is important.

Please note that this form is available online at:
www.GREATstaffrecognition.com/bookbonus/DIYforms
You have permission to print it for your use to conduct this recognition research.

G enuine
R elevant
E xplicit
A ppropriate
T imely

Chapter 5
If I Do Everything Well,
I Must Do a Good Job of Something!

Imagine receiving a note that read:

"Thank you for nothing in particular!"

Not really words to make someone feel special, are they? It's unlikely that you could purchase a card with this message in your local greeting card shop, but I once spied a card pinned to a bulletin board that basically conveyed the same message:

"Thank you for everything you do!"

It had come from staff in another department to the staff of a copy centre of a medium-sized organization. The people in the other department were obviously pleased with the service they had received. But why? What had the copy centre staff done?

Vague expressions of appreciation have limited value. While the sentiments behind the card being sent were **Genuine**, the message failed to identify what the copy-centre staff had done to prompt the thank you. Without a clear picture of what the other staff appreciated, how could they know what to do again?

The message of appreciation would have been stronger had it come with **Explicit** description of what the copy-centre staff had done:

- "Thank you for getting the report to us so quickly."
- "We liked your suggestion that we print the appendix on different coloured paper. It made the report easier for our clients to understand."
- "Your suggestion that we double-side the project saved paper and reduced our mailing costs. Thank you."

 "Recognition strategies are a systematic way of reinforcing behaviors, activities and results that you want repeated."
— Kathe M. Farris, *recognition consultant*

Explicit Feedback Makes Your Expectations Clear

Most job descriptions are collections of generalizations and vague statements of expectations. There is not enough information to enable employees to do their jobs effectively. More is required.

When supervisors explicitly describe what they appreciate about staff members' performance, they clarify job expectations. By identifying and praising when someone does something that contributes to success on the job, supervisors communicate what is important on the job.

They are setting the criteria for success. The feedback confirms for recipients that they are doing what is expected of them. This increases the likelihood that the desired behaviour will be repeated. When delivered publicly, **Explicit** recognition reminds everyone of the expectations. Employees can incorporate the positive feedback into their jobs. With a better understanding of what is expected and valued, they are able to respond to the needs of customers and co-workers more effectively.

Recognition linked to job expectations also provides the basis for self-recognition. Every time a staff member repeats actions for which she was recognized, she may recall what was said and how it made her feel. The memory may be enough to spark a moment of private celebration of her success.

Some employees seem blind to their own strengths and successes. Recognition that focuses on what was done well helps them discover their strengths, and what is valued by the organization. They may be inspired to repeat their behaviour.

Small Things that Make the Big Things Possible

Managers and supervisors can easily become caught up in the big picture. They only see the outcomes, reflected in the number of widgets produced, student scores on exams or sales figures. What they can miss are the small contributions and struggles that lead to these outcomes. Understanding and reinforcing the right behaviours that lead to the right results can increase the quality of those results.

To provide **Explicit** recognition a supervisor needs to understand what he wants to see more of, and commit to reinforcing this behaviour when he sees it. This means focusing on the small things that make the job easier, improve the work climate, or bring joy to the workplace.

Explicit recognition demands attention to detail. It requires close contact between supervisors and the staff they supervise. Supervisors who deliver **Explicit** recognition demonstrate that they are paying attention. They are seen as caring about staff members and knowing what they are doing. Supervisors who spend their days in their offices will find it difficult to provide **Explicit** recognition.

While general "thanks-for-everything" recognition alone is meaningless, if it's rooted in **Explicit** statements it can be powerful. Describe what the person did that led to the general recognition.

"George, I appreciate the insight you brought to our discussion of that problem. After listening to what others had been saying, you summarized the conversation in a way that made the solution obvious. Your thoughtful approach makes our business successful."

Generalized positive feedback raises questions in people's mind: "What did I do? How can I do it again?" Answer both questions with **Explicit** recognition.

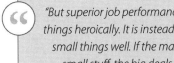

"But superior job performance is not a matter of doing a few things heroically. It is instead a matter of doing a great many small things well. If the manager provides recognition for small stuff, the big deals will take care of themselves."
— **Dick Grote, *Discipline Without Punishment***

At Least 3 Ways to Deliver
Explicit Recognition

1. General praise may be appreciated, but it doesn't last. Describe what the staff member did that you appreciated—and would like to see repeated. When did the praise-worthy event occur and what did the person do? Be sure to use her name.

2. Use the SAR formula:
   Situation – A description of the circumstances or challenge the employee faced
   Action – What the individual did to address the circumstances
   Results – What happened as a result of the action taken, how this relates to the success of the organization or individual

   (Adapted from *How to Choose the Right Person for the Right Job Every Time* by Lori Davila and Louise Kursmark (Toronto: McGraw Hill, 2005) ISBN 0071431233

   See Chapter 27, "Doing Recognition Right," for more formulas to make recognition meaningful—and **Explicit**.

3. Being **Explicit** allows you to praise an underachieving employee for some small thing he does well, or for small performance improvements. A general "great job" would be inappropriate and dishonest. And just maybe, your positive words will motivate additional improvement.

"Be careful what [behaviour] you reinforce because you will get more of it."
— Aubrey Daniels,
"the father of performance management"

G	enuine
R	elevant
E	xplicit
A	ppropriate
T	imely

Chapter 6

Not All Women Love to Shop

Content Warning

The following attempt at staff recognition was premised on gender stereotyping. Like most stereotypes, this one proved to be wrong.

Sometimes, things don't work the way they are supposed to. What seemed like a good idea at the time proves not to be. Such was the case a few years ago when I had the opportunity to implement a staff recognition idea I came across in my reading.

A client had hired a new human resources manager, but due to contractual obligations elsewhere, the manager was unable to take up his new duties for a few months. To provide coverage during this interval, I was invited to oversee the department. While in this role, I worked closely with three talented women on whose knowledge and experience I came to rely.

When the new manager was in place and my contract was ending, I wanted to do something special to say thank you to these women who had been so helpful. The new manager agreed to my request that I take them for an "extended lunch." I met the three at a local restaurant.

The food was tasty and the conversation pleasant. During the meal, I expressed my appreciation for their help and support during the months we had worked together. When I paid the bill, the women took this as a signal that it was time to return to work and prepared to leave.

But it wasn't time for them to return to work just yet. I had one more thing planned for them. I placed an envelope on the table in front of each woman. Each contained a small amount of cash.

One woman began to thank me for the gift, but I stopped her.

"This money comes with strings attached," I said. I explained that they were to go to a nearby mall where they would have one hour to spend their money, but there were conditions:

- they could only spend the money on something for themselves
- what they spent could not exceed the amount of money that they had just received
- any leftover money would be donated to a charity that was being supported by the employees in their office

As they left for the mall, I frankly was feeling pretty smug about what I was doing. What a perfect way to recognize staff! Three women…able to go shopping…for themselves…with someone else's money…on company time. What could be more perfect?

As agreed, we met in the mall's food fair an hour later. One by one, each woman revealed her purchases, before surrendering any unspent cash.

The first had purchased an inexpensive watch and a blouse. She returned a few dollars for the charity. The next had purchased a sweater and some perfume. Because both items had been on sale, she had a little more money left over for charity than her colleague.

The third women hesitated before showing us what she had bought. When I saw the contents of her shopping bag, my first thought was that these were the types of things I would have purchased if I had been told to go shopping for myself. No clothing. No jewelry. No perfume. She had used the money to buy three CDs and two books. She also had enough cash leftover to more than double what I had collected from the other two women.

"I really don't like shopping for myself," she confessed.

The Perils of Not Knowing Individuals Well Enough
While she understood what I had tried to do, it was clear that what I had done was not an **Appropriate** way to express appreciation to this woman. I was guilty of not knowing her well enough to understand how best to recognize her contributions to my success. Without this knowledge, I had simply copied what someone else had done to recognize staff, without pausing to

consider if the technique would be **Appropriate** for those who I wished to thank. Worse yet, I had allowed myself to be influenced by gender stereotyping: i.e. all women love to go shopping.

The painful lesson was that staff recognition that works for one—or most—doesn't necessarily work for all. Recognition is most effective when the recipient is recognized in a way that is meaningful to her. How we express appreciation—whether with a thank-you card, a plaque, a small gift, an invitation to lunch, or time off—will work only if the gesture matches the recognition preferences of the recipient.

> "Some want to be recognized by you, 'the boss.' Others see their peers as the truest source of recognition. Others crave their praise on a public stage. Others shun the glare of publicity, valuing only that quiet, private word of thanks."
> — **Marcus Buckingham and Curt Coffman,** *First, Break All the Rules*

Frequently, this is not the way it happens. When deciding how to recognize someone, the supervisor fails to consider, or doesn't even know, what recognition would be **Appropriate** for the recipient. The decision is based on the preferences of the person delivering the recognition. She chooses to recognize others in a way that reflects the type of recognition she values. This may be how she has been recognized in the past or would prefer to be recognized in the future. Gifts or tokens used to show appreciation reflect the giver's interests or values. The recognizer thinks, "This is how I would like to be recognized. It would motivate me; so it will work for others."

Such thinking can lead to some disastrous staff recognition moments, such as giving:

- a bottle of wine to a non-drinker or recovering alcoholic
- a golf pass for someone who shares Mark Twain's view that, "Golf is a good walk spoiled."
- tickets to an event scheduled in a distant city where the company's head office is located
- a certificate presented to a shy person in front of her colleagues
- an Easter ham given to a Muslim or vegetarian
- extra time off to someone who never uses all of his vacation time

One-Size Recognition Doesn't Work

Decisions can also be influenced by a desire to be fair when recognizing staff. This might lead to a belief that there should be no appearance of playing favourites. Therefore, all staff will be recognized in the same way, without regard to the significance of their individual contributions or achievements, or their recognition preferences.

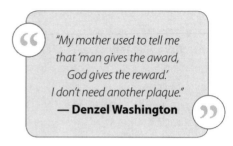

> *"My mother used to tell me that 'man gives the award, God gives the reward.' I don't need another plaque."*
> — **Denzel Washington**

Supervisors who feel this way seek the perfect staff recognition tool. They believe there is one technique that will meet their staff recognition needs for all staff, under all circumstances. Those who are convinced they have found the right tool feel that everyone one will:

- enjoy being called up in front of their peers to receive another certificate or wall plaque
- feel appreciated and motivated when they receive a baseball cap or vest emblazoned with the company logo
- be proud of where they work if they are given a paperweight for their desk or an inspirational poster for the wall

The belief that there is a single, best way to recognize has led companies to spend a great deal of money on recognition trinkets that seldom convey messages of appreciation successfully. Items bearing the company logo are often never used or worn. They are thrown into the back of closets where they remain until discovered years later when the closet is being cleaned out prior to a garage sale or a visit to a charity's clothing donation box. What was purchased to recognize staff is not **Appropriate** for the eventual recipients. How people are being recognized does not match how they prefer to be recognized.

The Desire to Be Seen as Unique

Recognition is a personal thing. It is most meaningful when the recipient values the gesture. When everyone is recognized in the same fashion, it feels as if the supervisor views everyone in the same way, as just another cog in the corporate machine. Employees feel that supervisors are focused just on what they do and not who they are as individuals. Most people want to be seen and treated as unique. They want to feel that their supervisors know who they are and what they do. They want to be acknowledged for how and what they contribute as individuals, not just as part of their work team. They want to be recognized in ways that are **Appropriate** to them.

When recognition is not **Appropriate**, it leaves the recipient feeling that the person providing the recognition doesn't know or care about him. Recognition that is inappropriate will not be valued by the recipient and will fail to motivate him to perform the same or similar tasks as well in the future. There may also be a spillover affect. Co-workers who are aware of what the recipient did and how he was recognized will not be

> *"What is sauce for the goose may be sauce for the gander but is not necessarily sauce for the chicken, the duck, the turkey or the guinea hen."*
> — **Alice B. Toklas, American writer**

motivated by this gesture to perform well. If the recognition was particularly inappropriate, the staff member may actually avoid doing something that might result in him enduring a similar experience in the future.

Discovering Uniqueness

Supervisors who do a good job of recognizing staff members appropriately believe that people are unique. Each has her own strengths and weaknesses, career and personal goals, and interests. Workforce diversity is more than just visible characteristics such as race and gender. Even in a workplace that outwardly appears homogeneous, there is great diversity within the group.

Appropriate recognition begins with supervisors knowing the people they supervise. This means simply knowing employees, being able to greet them by name, and committing to learning something about each individual. The better a supervisor knows each staff member, the easier it is to personalize recognition for each individual.

When supervisors recognize in ways that reflect staff members' recognition preferences, it shows they care about staff members as individuals. When the effort is made to provide **Appropriate** recognition, the recognition appears more **Genuine**.

> *"The more personalized the praise, the more the receiver knows it is well thought out and carefully considered. Personalized praise lets people know they are recognized as special and unique."*
> — **Sharon F. Marks, It Pays to Praise**

65

A supervisor is better able to personalize recognition when she understands the staff member's career goals, how he spends his spare time, what he likes best (or least) about his job, the religious and cultural holidays he observes, and how he likes to be recognized.

A supervisor can learn more about individual staff members in several ways. The simplest, most straightforward way is to ask—either during face-to-face conversations or with the use of a questionnaire. Some supervisors may feel uncomfortable asking these questions of people with whom they have worked for some time. You shouldn't be, if you are clear about why you are asking. Most staff members will appreciate that you care enough to want to learn what makes them unique. After gathering information from existing staff about their interests and how they like to be recognized, the same questions can be part of the process as new staff is brought on-board.

Another way to learn about staff is to apply the observational skills of a detective. Look for clues throughout the workplace. What does the staff member talk about when he has a choice, such as during breaks (hobbies, sports, community involvement)? What does he laugh about? What does he eat at break time? What does he doodle during meetings? What type of tasks does he prefer to do?

Visit each employee's workplace. What does she display in her work area that reflects her hobbies and interests? Is this someone who displays certificates, plaques, or trophies? Are there photos of family members or friends? Are there mementoes of special events or vacations? To make this aspect of your investigation easier, encourage staff to personalize their work areas with family photos and any things that are important to them.

Besides making your own observations, talk to others about the employee. Co-workers, family and friends can all offer insights. They may be able to confirm conclusions you have made, based on your observations, and provide additional insights that will help you recognize each staff member more appropriately.

"The capacity for delight is the gift of paying attention."
— Julia Cameron, *American poet and novelist*

As you strive to make recognition more **Appropriate,** observe how each staff member responds to recognition. Does he seem comfortable being recognized in public, or does he seem to avoid public recognition? What does he do with tokens of appreciation such as certificates, trophies or small gifts? Staff recognition techniques have a limited shelf life. What worked well in the past may have become less meaningful over time. Be sensitive to this. Look for signs that techniques that once worked are becoming stale and that new approaches are needed.

Recognition becomes **Appropriate** when it is chosen based on the interests and personality of the recipient. When recognition is **Appropriate,** it has greater value for the recipient. The message of appreciation is stronger.

When Making Recognition Appropriate is Inappropriate

As important as it is that the recipient finds the recognition **Appropriate**, there is a caveat. The search for recognition that is **Appropriate** to the individual may lead to practices that are unacceptable to the organization. Individual recognition needs must align with the organization's values and be consistent with community norms. Government-funded agencies must not be seen as misusing public money. Private-sector companies must engage in recognition practices that are acceptable to shareholders.

Questions to Get to Know Staff Members Better

The key to providing **Appropriate** recognition is to know the people with whom you work as individuals. These questions will help you learn about them. You wouldn't ask all these questions at any one time—and there may be questions that would be inappropriate for your workplace—but you could keep some in mind during one-on-one conversations, or when preparing a questionnaire for existing and new staff. The answers will help you get to know staff members better. The better you know them, the better able you are to personalize the recognition you provide.

Personal

- How do you like to spend your spare time? What are your hobbies, interests and passions?
- If you had a day when you were free to do anything, how would you spend it?
- How do you like to relax?
- What makes you smile?
- What magazines do you read?
- What was your best vacation ever? What made it so good?
- If you could go anywhere on vacation, where would you go?
- What is your favourite colour? Favourite season? Favourite flower?
- What is your favourite day of the week? Why?
- Where do you like to go on a day out with your family or friends?
- What type of volunteer work do you do in the community?
- What charities do you support?
- Do you belong to a service club? Which one?
- What are your favourite places to shop?
- In which store are you most likely to max out your credit card?
- What is your favourite pet (real or imaginary)?
- What type of car do you dream of driving?
- What is your birthday (year optional)?
- What are the names and birthdates of members of your immediate family?
- What holidays do you celebrate during the year?

Work/Career

- What are some "high-five" moments in your work life?
- What kind of projects do you like to work on?
- What do you like most about your job? What are your job frustrations?
- How could we make your job more satisfying?
- What would you like to learn more about?
- What are your career goals?
- How do you prefer others to communicate with you—face-to-face, via email, telephone, or text?

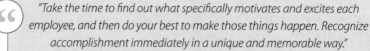

> *"Take the time to find out what specifically motivates and excites each employee, and then do your best to make those things happen. Recognize accomplishment immediately in a unique and memorable way."*
> **— Bob Nelson, "Secrets of Successful Employee Recognition"**

Recognition
- How would you like to be recognized for doing your job well?
- How do you feel about being recognized in public? Would you prefer to be recognized in private?
- In what way would you prefer that we communicate with you?
  ❑ email ❑ face-to-fac ❑ voice mail ❑ in writing

Food
- What is your favourite snack (anything you eat or drink between meals)?
- What is your favourite sweet treat? Salty treat?
- What is your favourite hot drink? Cold drink?
- How do you like your coffee? With sugar? With cream?
- How do you like your tea? With sugar? With honey? With milk?
- What is your favourite restaurant for an evening out with your significant other?
- What is your favourite fast food restaurant?
- What is your favourite fast food to eat?
- What toppings do you like on pizza?
- What is your favourite type of wine (red, white, bubbly, dry, sweet)?
- What dietary restrictions or food allergies do you have?

Entertainment
- What type of music do you like to listen to?
- Who are your favourite recording artists?
- What types of movies do you enjoy watching?
- What are some of your favourite movies of all time?
- Who are your favourite movie or television actors?
- What are some of your favourite television shows (current or past)?
- Which sports teams do you support?
- What type of concerts do you like to attend?
- Who are your favourite athletes?
- Who are your favourite authors?
- Who is your favourite cartoon character?
- What is your favourite song ("theme song for life")?

At Least 14 Ways to Use What You Learn About Employees to Make Recognition Appropriate

1. Respect the individual's preference for public or private recognition whenever possible.
2. When food is part of your recognition plans, offer treats or food that match the individual's preferences. Take him for lunch at his favourite restaurant.
3. Make a donation in the employee's name to the charity of her choice. When the charity sends her a thank-you, or someone asks why her employer made the donation, it will enhance your expression of gratitude for her efforts.
4. Say something positive to employees on their birthdays or the anniversary of their employment.
5. Buy a staff member a book that he was planning to read, or one by his favourite author.
6. When you know which charities employees support, you can invite them to bring an information display about the organization into the workplace, or provide time off to volunteer with the charity.
7. Assign tasks that will help the employee grow professionally and work toward her career goals.
8. Have a grab bag of trinkets on your desk. Invite those you are recognizing to select something from your collection.
9. Invite team members to spend a few minutes describing their hobbies or outside interests to their co-workers.
10. Offer recognition in the form of lessons that relate to the staff member's interest, be it golf, sewing, cooking or fitness.
11. Before recognizing someone in public, play a song by his favourite artist.
12. In a diverse workplace, learn to say thank you in the native language of each staff member . . . and then say it.
13. Give a deserving staff member a mug filled with her favourite treats.
14. Present a staff member with a signed and framed photograph of his favourite sports hero or movie star.

 "If you talk to a man in a language he understands, that goes to his head. If you talk to him in his language, that goes to his heart."
— Nelson Mandela, *South African statesman*

DIY RECOGNITION RESEARCH:
Appropriate Recognition for Whom?

What you will need for this research project:
Yourself, your work team

Research Process:
1. From the following list, identify what you think are the four best ways to recognize staff.

   ☐ Cash bonus
   ☐ Small gift
   ☐ Email message of thanks
   ☐ Time off
   ☐ Article in the staff newsletter
   ☐ Announcement of my contribution or achievement at a staff meeting
   ☐ Acknowledgement by a co-worker
   ☐ Note of commendation placed in my personnel file
   ☐ Letter from my supervisor
   ☐ A few words of thanks from my supervisor
   ☐ A plaque or certificate of accomplishment
   ☐ Handwritten thank-you note
   ☐ Letter from my supervisor's boss
   ☐ Being nominated for a company-wide award
   ☐ Other: _____

2. Give a copy of the same list to each staff member. Ask each individual to identify the four ways in which they would prefer to be recognized.
3. Compare the lists.

Implications for the Workplace:
Are you recognizing staff in ways they wish to be recognized?

Hint: Different people prefer to be recognized in different ways. No single staff recognition technique will work for everyone. There is no staff recognition equivalent of a multi-tool. Or Swiss Army knife.

G enuine
R elevant
E xplicit
A ppropriate
T imely

Chapter 7
Recognition Delayed is Recognition Diminished

When is the best time to recognize staff members for doing their jobs well? Ideally, while the performance that warrants recognition is still going on.

This is best exemplified in the world of professional athletes and performers. The hometown quarterback drops back and unleashes a long pass. Thousands of fans leap to their feet as the receiver reaches up, pulls in the football and turns up field. The cheering grows louder as he gets closer to the end zone. The roar of the crowd becomes deafening as the hero of the moment crosses the goal line. Another six points for the home team.

Meanwhile, across town, a famous recording artist steps on to the stage. Applause. She strums the first notes of her greatest hit. More applause fills the concert hall.

While the cheers and applause may be loudest when the concert concludes or the hometown team emerges victorious, these professionals don't have to wait to experience the appreciation of fans. Why then, should the

"Swift gratitude is the sweetest."
— Greek proverb

people who work for your organization—all professionals in their fields— have to wait until some time in the future, perhaps the distant future, to hear applause for what they do? They are just as deserving of words of encouragement throughout their "performances" as professional athletes and recording artists.

Back at the office, feedback can also be immediate. As she passes, a supervisor overhears an employee solving a particularly difficult problem for a customer who is obviously happy with the solution. Catching the employee's eye, the supervisor gives the employee a big smile and a thumbs-up. Immediately, the employee knows that how he handled the situation is appreciated.

Later the same day, the supervisor overhears another employee responding to a phone inquiry, guiding the customer through the troubleshooting procedure related to a computer program the customer had just purchased. This time, she gives the staff member a nod. Before she returns to her office, the supervisor passes by the staff member's desk. There she pauses long enough to write a brief message on a sticky note, which she attaches to the employee's computer: "Thanks! **GREAT** Job!"

Integrating Recognition Into One's Daily Routine

In both examples, the supervisor is available to provide **Timely** recognition because she has made a point of leaving her office to spend time in the area where staff members are dealing with customers. She is there for a purpose: to see what staff members are doing, and as often as possible, to catch them doing it well. When she does, she ensures that they know she saw and appreciates what they did.

This supervisor has integrated recognition into her daily work routine. As she moves around the office, she is conscientiously searching for employees who are doing their jobs well. When she sees good behaviour, she responds spontaneously. There is an element of surprise in recognition that is **Timely.** Employees don't know when recognition will occur. The supervisor has harnessed the power of the unexpected. While it is nice to receive recognition when it is expected, such as for a service anniversary, gestures of appreciation become special when they are unexpected. It is the difference between a birthday gift that arrives on schedule and a gift that arrives on a Tuesday afternoon, "just because."

Like the cheering fans in a sports stadium, supervisors who provide immediate recognition demonstrate their awareness–and appreciation–for what is happening. Working in a workplace without recognition is like performing music in a concert hall filled with a tone-deaf audience.

 "We should give as we would receive, cheerfully, quickly and without hesitation; for there is no grace in a benefit that sticks to the fingers."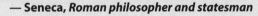
— **Seneca, Roman philosopher and statesman**

There is no benefit to storing up several examples of positive behaviour to release a torrent of recognition during a special "recognition event," which may be weeks or months away. When recognition is given months after the event, it appears contrived and does little to motivate the recipient to repeat the behaviour or achieve similar outcomes. When recognition is delayed until the "right" time, it appears that it was scheduled for the convenience of the presenter, not for the recipient's need to be recognized in a **Timely** fashion. To make recognition meaningful, we have to take time now to recognize people.

Formal Recognition is Often Recognition Delayed

Formal recognition programs can be cumbersome. They often require mountains of paperwork and months to process. First, someone nominates another for an award. The nomination is submitted to a committee that meets only occasionally to scrutinize the nominations. By the time a decision is made and is communicated to the nominator, so much water has passed under the bridge that neither the nominator nor nominee can fully remember the incident that prompted the nomination.

Some time ago, a teacher with whom I worked was nominated for an Excellence in Teaching Award. The process of vetting the nominations was lengthy, requiring several months to complete. While nominations were submitted during one school year, the awards themselves were not announced and presented until the fall of the next school year.

She was an exemplary teacher and few were surprised when she was among 20 winners who were invited to attend an awards dinner with the minister of education. But going to the dinner turned out to be somewhat awkward. Over the intervening summer break, the teacher had left the classroom to attend graduate school several provinces across the country. The things for which she was being recognized were now part of a former life.

The Importance of Timely Recognition

There is a strong business case for **Timely** recognition. Immediate feedback reinforces that what was observed is what is expected and appreciated. Staff members do not have to puzzle about what is valued, or experiment with other approaches in hope of discovering what is important to their supervisors. The more immediate the feedback, the more likely the desired behaviour will be repeated. The sooner the recognition, the fresher the memory of what was done is in the mind of both the giver and the recipient. Being able to recall what she did, the employee is more likely to repeat the behaviour. When the recognition is **Timely,** there is a stronger emotional connection between the behaviour and the appreciation. Most people will want to repeat behaviour that leads to a positive emotional experience.

It isn't always possible to provide immediate recognition. To do so would mean interrupting the flow of the employee's work. In these cases, a supervisor should make a mental note to follow up with the individual as soon as possible, either in person or with a brief note. Writing that thank-you note could be added to tomorrow's to-do list to ensure it is not overlooked.

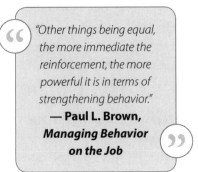

"Other things being equal, the more immediate the reinforcement, the more powerful it is in terms of strengthening behavior."
— **Paul L. Brown,**
Managing Behavior on the Job

Other times, the supervisor may not observe first-hand what the employee is doing. He may only become aware of the employee's good work after it's completed. Maybe it will reach him in the form of a well-written report or a sales record. Sometimes the supervisor may learn about the employee's actions through a note or phone call from a customer, or from a co-worker's comment. To ensure **Timely** recognition, the supervisor should express appreciation soon after he becomes aware of what the individual has achieved or how she contributed. Recognition may come in the form of a conversation, during which the supervisor asks the employee to describe what she did to achieve the results that attracted the supervisor's attention. Most people are proud to describe their successes.

Performance Appraisals: A Poor Time to Recognize

The worst time to recognize staff may be during their annual performance appraisals. This is not a time to offer fresh feedback, either positive or negative. The rule for performance appraisals should be, no surprises. Feedback should be given on an ongoing basis, and the annual appraisal meeting should be a time to summarize what has already been said over the past months and to set goals.

Not only will the details of events that occurred months ago have been largely forgotten, but staff members may not be as receptive to positive feedback during a performance assessment as they might be at another time. Most approach these meetings with some trepidation, expecting to hear bad news. When positive feedback is heard for the first time within the context of a performance appraisal, it is easy for the employee to dismiss these comments as just a buffer against the bad news yet to come. Anticipating that the immediate future will hold negative messages, the employee is unlikely to listen carefully to the words of appreciation, let alone remember them.

Performance appraisals themselves are often overlooked as a form of recognition. When supervisors stick to the schedule, providing formal feedback when it is expected, this shows that they value the employees enough to offer **Timely** feedback. Well-conducted performance appraisals both assess what the staff member has done and point out ways the employee can improve and build on his strengths. Most staff wants feedback. They don't want to guess how they're doing. Some may interpret a delayed performance appraisal as a sign that their supervisor is dissatisfied with their work, but reluctant to confront them. Without any feedback from the supervisor, they begin to invent performance problems and worry that these imagined shortcomings are seen by others.

Other employees see the lack of feedback as evidence that their supervisors don't care about them. Whether caused by worry or a feeling that no one cares, the results will be the same: declining morale and productivity—and the start of a new job search. When it comes to the failure to provide performance appraisals as scheduled, no news is seldom seen as good news.

Even though the impact of recognition declines as time passes, there is no statute of limitations on staff recognition. Recognition delayed is better than no recognition at all, as long as the feeling of appreciation is **Genuine,** and the act of recognition includes at least one of the other components of meaningful recognition—it is **Relevant, Explicit** or **Appropriate.**

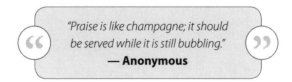

"Praise is like champagne; it should be served while it is still bubbling."
— **Anonymous**

At Least 7 Ways to Keep Recognition Timely

1. Keep track of when and how often you recognize members of your staff. If you haven't recognized a person in the past week, recognition is overdue.

2. Create a collection of on-the-spot recognition items, consisting of items that make immediate recognition possible: thank-you cards, sticky notes, stickers, candies and coupons for special awards, such as an extra coffee or a free snack in the company cafeteria.

3. Schedule time each day for staff recognition. Think about the people you work with. Who has done something in the past couple of days that made your job easier, moved the department closer to its goals, or reflected the values of the organization? Thank them.

4. Spend time each day on the front line to catch staff doing well. Let them know what you saw them do and why you appreciate it.

5. Acknowledge staff when recognition isn't expected, not just at recognition events, during staff meetings, or when a project ends.

6. Practise "walk-by" staff recognition. As you move about your office, hospital, school, or across the shop floor, be alert for staff doing things well…for good performance in progress. When you see it, let the employee know that you have seen it. Give him a thumbs-up, a nod of acknowledgement, a smile, or a few words of appreciation. Recognition is best when it is timely. It's timely when it is delivered while whatever is being recognized is still happening.

7. Ensure service awards are presented when they are due, rather than months or even years after they have been earned. This is especially important when the presentation occurs at the department level, rather than during a corporate-wide event.

8. Conduct performance reviews as prescribed. Nothing says, "I don't care about you," more than delaying for months, or never telling staff how they are doing.

 "Do it now. It is not safe to leave a generous feeling to the cooling influences of the world."
— Thomas Guthrie,
Scottish clergyman and philanthropist

Excuses, Rationalizations and Cop-outs (Part II)

"We show our appreciation every two weeks when people get their pay-cheques. What else do they expect?"

A paycheque is what a person gets just for doing the job. It arrives regularly, whether the employee's performance is outstanding or merely adequate. A paycheque should never be equated with showing appreciation. Salary, wages and benefits may all attract workers, but what keeps them—and keeps them engaged, productive and committed—is knowing that what they are doing is valued by their supervisor.

Financial health is important to us all. Money pays the rent, puts food on the table and clothes on our back. Praise and recognition nourishes us emotionally. Recognition is the something extra. Like dessert after a meal of meat and potatoes; the icing on the cake.

"If I recognize them once, they'll expect more recognition. They will be spoiled by recognition and become complacent."

You're half right. Recognize someone for doing something well and the next time he does something well he may expect you to say something. If what you recognize him for is something that is **Relevant** to your organization's mission, what's wrong with this? If he is doing what you want him to do, why wouldn't you want to express your appreciation again…and again… and again?

Will too much recognition spoil people and make them complacent? Will the impact of recognition be lost? I don't think so. I have never met anyone who complained: "I don't know what's wrong with my supervisor. Every day it's the same. I do something and there she is, telling me how well I've done and that I am appreciated for what I do. I hate coming to work to hear all these positives! I don't want to do anything anymore, because if I do, she'll just praise me again."

"It is just that other things are more important to people [than money]. I have done hundreds and hundreds of sessions where I have an activity that asks people to think about the last time they were appreciated. No one ever thinks of the number on his or her paycheque. They think of someone who took the time and effort to say or do something after they had success."
— **Bob Nelson,** *author*

What I do hear is complaints that, "no one appreciates me for how hard I work. I wish they would say thank you once in a while." Nearly a third of those surveyed in a study by The Gallup Organization reported that they had not been recognized even once in the previous 12 months.

Have you ever wondered what supervisors who seldom or never recognize staff at work are like at home? How often do they tell their spouses that they love them? Once a year on their anniversary…if they remember? How well do you think that is working for them?

As long as it is **Genuine** and focused on contributions that are **Relevant** to the organization fulfilling its mission and meeting its goals, recognition remains meaningful to its recipients. The more frequent it is, the better.

"Employee neglect is an organization's silent killer, a malignancy that will eat away its very core. I believe strategic recognition of your employees is instrumental in reducing turnover, increasing productivity and creating a positive work environment. In order for an organization to achieve success its employees must embrace the organization's mission, goals and values. This can only happen when employees realize their contributions are important and integral to their organization's success."
— Christi Gibson, *executive director of Recognition Management Institute, producer of Recognition Radio (www.Rideau.com), and former executive director, Recognition Professionals International*

"Employees don't want to be singled out for recognition. It embarrasses them."
You are right—for some people, some of the time.

Different people like to be recognized in different ways. Some don't like to be recognized publicly in front of others, while others love it. It is important to know your staff and to understand their individual recognition preferences. What type of recognition is **Appropriate** for each person? This is something you will learn. Through trial and error, or through discussion with individuals, you will discover how best to personalize the recognition you provide.

Recipients are unlikely to be embarrassed if recognition is delivered appropriately and in ways that are consistent with their recognition preferences.

"It's not in the budget."

Staff recognition is much more about attitude than costly tokens of appreciation. If you genuinely wish to express appreciation to staff, there are many ways to do so at little or no cost. This and other books on staff recognition are filled with low-cost, no-cost staff recognition ideas.

Some managers are reluctant to waste money on something as frivolous as staff recognition. They don't want to divert funds from the key purpose of the organization—educating children, caring for the ill, building widgets, serving restaurant meals or providing necessary social services. In reality, a few dollars spent on meaningful recognition may actually reduce what needs to be spent to attract customers, or to recruit people to replace staff who resign for jobs elsewhere.

Advertising may attract customers, but businesses need pleasant, engaged and knowledgeable staff to keep them. Employees who are unmotivated and disinterested can easily drive customers away. Staff members who feel unappreciated will be more focused on pursuing job possibilities elsewhere. Every time an existing staff member is lured away by another job, you are faced with the expense of hiring someone new.

Customer-service experts estimate it takes six to 10 times as much effort to attract a new customer as it would take to keep an existing customer. I suggest that the same is true of staff, our "internal customers." A few dollars spent today to retain current staff may reduce future recruitment costs. Keeping staff, and keeping them focused on the organization's goals, will also contribute to keeping customers longer, something that may allow you to reduce your advertising budget.

"Many times, we are asked, 'How much will an effective recognition system cost us and what is the return on investment?' When you consider that the majority of your employees are not working up to their potential, the more important questions would be, 'How much is it costing you NOT to have an effective recognition system?' "

— Sue Glasscock and Kimberly Gram,
Workplace Recognition

"If I show them any appreciation they will expect a pay increase."
There are supervisors who fear that words spoken in praise will come back to haunt them during an employee's annual performance appraisal. They believe that employees will quote what the supervisor said and demand a big raise.

This is unlikely. Money is more likely to become an issue when staff feels unappreciated. In the absence of other signs of appreciation, money becomes a poor substitute for **Genuine** praise as evidence of the employee's value to the organization. "Show me that you appreciate me; show me the money!" People who are happy and engaged in their work and feel valued for what they do, are less likely to complain about what they are being paid.

This does not mean that if you are good at recognition that you can get away with paying your staff a lot less than they would earn elsewhere. Good workers should be compensated fairly. People need to be able to meet their basic needs for food, clothing and shelter. Once these physiological needs are satisfied, and they have a sense of security, people start to look for more from the job. They begin to look for ways to fulfill their needs for social relationships and self-esteem. These higher-level needs are better met in a work environment characterized by a culture of recognition.

"Money is not the most important consideration for people at work. The way people are treated at work is much more important for determining performance than the money they receive."
— Audrey C. Daniels,
Bringing Out the Best in People:
How to Apply the Astonishing Power
of Positive Reinforcement

DIY RECOGNITION RESEARCH: Creating That Good Feeling

What you will need for this research project:
A small piece of sandpaper, a cotton ball, your face

Research Process:
1. Hold the sandpaper in one hand and the cotton ball in the other. Gently rub one side of your face with the sandpaper and the other side with the cotton ball. Which feels better?

2. Repeat. This time, rub a little harder. Which feels better this time?

3. If you were to rub your face again, but with only the sandpaper or cotton ball, which would you choose?

Caution: As with any physical activity, you should consult a physician before you begin this activity. If you select the sandpaper over the cotton ball to rub your face the final time, we recommend that you that consult a psychiatrist before continuing.

Implications for the Workplace:
What is the nature of the feedback you provide? Is it negative feedback (sandpaper)—pointing out what your staff does wrong in hopes they will do it right the next time? Or is it mainly positive feedback (cotton ball)—noting what they do well, so that they are encouraged to continue to do so?

Which do you think likely feels best? Which type of feedback is most likely to motivate them?

Hint: Staff will feel better—and be more engaged—when the feedback they receive is mainly positive.

SECTION THREE
Insights and Inspiration
from Unlikely Sources

Chapter 8
Nearly Everything I Really Needed to Know About Staff Recognition I Learned From My Dog

Exercise is important for good health and fitness. We all know that. Getting fit is near the top of most annual lists of resolutions. North Americans spend billions each year on fitness equipment. As happens with most New Year's resolutions, our commitment to fitness fades soon after the exercise equipment is purchased. Almost-new treadmills and stationary bicycles sit idle and ignored in basements and storage rooms. Their main workout value is the exertion owners put into dragging them up the stairs to be sold at their next garage sale.

Kojak was the only dog I ever owned. He was an extremely hairy, 100-pound border collie/German shepherd cross that shared his name with the 1970s TV detective played by a very bald Telly Savalas. He was better than any piece of exercise equipment I ever owned. While it may be easy to ignore an inanimate treadmill or exercise bike, it was not so easy to ignore a large, active dog that knew it was time for his walk.

"A dog is the only exercise machine that you cannot decide to skip when you don't feel like doing it."
— Carolyn G. Heilbrun,
American academic and author

For several years, meeting this need meant spending 45 minutes, morning and evening, rain or shine, from +30°C or -35°C, on the trails near where we lived in Fort McMurray, Alberta. Kojak and I often found ourselves alone on routes more frequented by deer, moose, black bears and foxes, than by other human beings or their pets. This solitude created opportunities for contemplation. It was also a time for Kojak to teach me lessons about people and their recognition needs.

Learning about people by observing dogs is nothing new. Ivan Pavlov, the Russian physiologist and Nobel laureate laid the groundwork for behavioural psychology through his experiments with dogs related to salivation and digestion.

When Pavlov presented food (an unconditioned stimulus), the dogs salivated (unconditioned response). Next, he combined the food with the sound of a bell (conditioned stimulus). Once the dogs had associated the ringing bell with food, they would salivate at the sound of the bell, alone. The promise (the ringing bell) of reward (food) was all that was needed to stimulate the desired behaviour (salivation).

Teachers and managers, alike, knowingly or unknowingly apply the principles of classic conditioning in their classrooms and workplaces to motivate students or workers. Work hard today and you will be rewarded (with a good report card, a raise or a promotion) in the future.

The routine of our walks didn't vary much from one day to the next. At the start, Kojak would stop to sniff trees to see who had passed that way recently and leave evidence that he, too, had been there—the canine equivalent of punching a time clock or signing a guest book. Later, he would wander off on his own to explore along the trail. As the walk progressed, he would appear at my left side from time to time, demonstrating the heeling position that he had learned when the two of us had enrolled in puppy kindergarten.

"Does the name Pavlov ring a bell?"
— Bumper sticker

Here was my first lesson:

Dogs will do what they believe we expect of them.

This was the behaviour that I had learned to reward (and Kojak had learned I would reward) during our obedience classes.

Having taken this position at my side, Kojak went through a series of behaviours, which if not interrupted with a treat or the unexpected appearance of a squirrel, always followed the same sequence.

At first, he seemed content to trot along at my side, eyes looking forward. After a short time, he would turn his head to look up at me expectantly, hopeful of making eye contact. Had I noticed how well he was heeling? Would I reward this desired behaviour?

If ignored, he would progress to the next phase. Still at my side, continuing to look up, he would emit a gentle growl. Not an angry growl; in fact, it was nearly inaudible. Just enough, he hoped, to catch my attention. Maybe I had not noticed how well he was heeling.

When there was still no response—I still hadn't reached into the pocket from which he had seen treats pulled before—Kojak would escalate things. Moving a couple steps ahead, he would turn to face me, and bark three times. "Surely, by now, you have noticed how well I have been heeling. I have done what you expect of me, now it is time for you to do what I expect of you."

Through this sequence, I discovered the second lesson:

Sometimes dogs will ask for feedback in the form of praise and reward when they know they have performed as expected.

When there was still no reward—likely because I had not remembered to refill my treat pocket—Kojak would once again return to heeling position, but only momentarily. Sensing that no reward would be coming, he would leave my side to explore in the nearby woods.

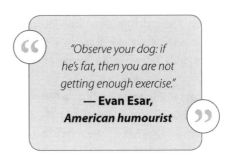

"Observe your dog: if he's fat, then you are not getting enough exercise."
— **Evan Esar,**
American humourist

I was left to contemplate the third lesson:

Ignore your dog and he will soon begin to ignore you.

As we returned home, Kojak and I would walk through an open field. If we both had energy, I would pick up a stick and toss it for the dog to retrieve. When he dropped it at my feet, I would give him a pat on the head, which was sometimes accompanied by a treat, before throwing the stick again. Having discovered that a retrieved stick would lead to a cookie, Kojak would chase a stick, even if he had not received a cookie the last time he retrieved the stick. There was always the promise of a cookie the next time …or the time after that. That anticipation is what Pavlov observed in his salivating dogs and what he labelled "conditioned stimulus."

As a young dog, Kojak would chase several sticks without receiving the cookie he anticipated. As he grew older, he seemed to grow wiser.

He would still chase a couple of sticks and return them with no more than a pat on the head as reward. But throw the stick the third time, and he would only watch it fly through the air before turning to look at you in a stance reminiscent of a defiant three-year-old, refusing to do what his mother asks.

"So! What are you going to do for me now that I have tracked down your stupid stick?"

Kojak had taught me a fourth lesson:

You can't fool an old dog with the same old tricks.

How Do These Lessons Apply To Recognizing The Performance Of Human Beings?

People are not dogs and should not be treated like dogs. But sometimes what we learn from dogs can guide how we treat people.

While it is easy to see how these observations may apply to dogs, how do some things that dogs do relate to people? When Kojak's lessons are re-worded, they can serve as a reminder of what most supervisors and managers already know about human nature.

Lesson #1: People will do what they believe we expect of them.

Just as dogs want to please their owners, staff want to please their supervisors by doing what they understand the supervisors want them to do. But how do employees learn what is important for on-the-job success?

This knowledge should come from managers and supervisors who should explain what is expected of staff when they first come to work for the orga-nization, and then remind them through regular feedback. Staff will be more productive and the organization more successful when expectations are clear.

In the absence of direction and feedback from supervisors, new employees will do what they believe is expected of them. These beliefs will be based on what others tell them they should do, what they see co-workers doing, how they handled similar tasks in previous jobs, or what they imagine is expected of them. Depending on the quality of the advice they receive, the appropriateness of behaviour they observe, and the relevance of their previous work experience and training, the beliefs they form based on these sources may or may not fit well with the employer's expectations.

A better way for employees to learn what is expected of them is by receiving recognition and seeing others recognized for doing the right things, the right way.

Lesson #2: Some employees will ask for feedback in the form of praise and recognition when they have performed their jobs well…and that's okay.
While ideally there should be few occasions when an individual feels the need to ask for feedback, that's not the way it is in many fast-paced work environments.

Supervisors may be unaware of each employee's contributions and achievements. In addition, the recognition needs of staff members vary. Some employees have a greater need for feedback than others. These indi-

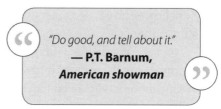

"Do good, and tell about it."
**— P.T. Barnum,
American showman**

viduals need to know that you are pleased with their performance and that they have your acceptance and support. This is necessary for them to maintain their self-esteem and self-confidence. Better that they ask for—and receive—feedback, than they interpret your silence as dissatisfaction with their performance. Too much worry about your assessment of their performance will distract them from performing well.

Few staff members will be as obvious as Kojak was—no growls, no barks. Their requests for praise and recognition will be more subtle, often taking the form of questions:

- "What did you think of the presentation I did for the board last week?"
- "Have you seen the sales figures for last month? What did you think?"
- "Did you like that idea?"
- "How do you feel about how I dealt with that upset customer?"
- "What can I do to make your job easier?"
- "I just completed my diploma at night school and will be graduating next week."

Supervisors and co-workers need to be alert to these requests and be prepared to respond appropriately. Lukewarm responses such as, "Oh, it was fine," or "Those figures seem all right," or "Yeah, you did okay," can be more painful than no feedback at all. The staff member will see the manager as disinterested in what she does and accomplishes—and indeed, in the employee herself. It is important to listen for the request behind the questions. Take time to listen, to look at something the staff member wants to show you, or to go with the employee to see what she is talking about.

Your response should reflect your true assessment of the individual's performance. If you were pleased, let the staff member know this, and why you feel as you do. If you feel the performance was not up to standard, let the employee know this, too. Include advice about how the employee's performance could be improved, and express your confidence that she will do a better job in the future.

For many employees, asking for recognition will be difficult. As a supervisor, you can make it easier by providing opportunities when it is easy to ask. When you meet with an employee one-on-one, visit a worksite, or encounter someone in the break room, you can create an opportunity for the employee to request recognition by asking, "What has gone well for you over the past couple of weeks?"

When the staff member mentions something, pick up on the theme:

- "I hadn't heard about that. Tell me more."
- "Wow! Sounds like you handled that well."
- "Why do you think it went so well?"

Lesson #3: Ignore your staff and they will soon begin to ignore you and your expectations.

Supervisors have a choice of three types of feedback they provide to employees. Positive feedback is the most effective type. It is the feedback that most staff members prefer—being told what they have done well and how much their contribution is appreciated. Positive feedback leads to enhanced self-esteem, improved morale and increased motivation—all of which lead to greater commitment and productivity.

Sometimes, when an employee's performance is inadequate, negative feedback is both deserved and appropriate. When given properly, negative feedback can lead to improved performance. Well-delivered negative feedback can even demonstrate that the supervisor cares about the employee and

How Do They Ask For Applause?

Think that no one asks for recognition? Think again. It happens every time we go to a sports event or concert.

No one is better at asking for applause than professional athletes and performers. And most aren't very subtle about it, either:

- A performer greets his audience with two simple words: "Hello [insert city's name here]!"
- The concert begins with the performer's greatest hit.
- The comedian inserts a local reference into one of his stock jokes—a local politician or celebrity, or a put-down of a rival city.
- Athletes on the field and on the bench wave their arms to encourage fans to cheer.
- A singer thrusts her arm into the air as a signal that the song is over and it's time to applaud.
- An athlete performs a victory dance after scoring.
- The performer praises the quality of the venue. "The acoustics here are so good. I love performing here."
- Someone on stage asks, "Are you having as much fun out there as we are having up here?"

Each gesture or comment is designed to elicit a response—applause, laughter, cheering.

Getting the audience involved in these ways is important to those on stage or the playing field. It creates an energy upon which they can build. No one wants to perform in front of a silent audience, with the possible exception of one of your teachers back in junior high school.

Your staff will also feed off the energy of regular applause. Unlike the professionals, they aren't as overt and proficient when making their requests. You will need to watch for subtle signs that staff members feel recognition is warranted.

If it's acceptable for professional athletes and performers to ask, shouldn't it be as acceptable for the professionals on your staff to ask for applause?

his development. To be effective, negative criticism must be constructive, focused on specific behaviour, and followed by an expression of confidence in the employee's ability to meet expectations.

Too much negative feedback—or only negative feedback—can be destructive. It can reduce people's self-esteem and self-confidence. Staff members' focus shifts from doing the job well to doing it well enough to avoid the boss's attention. "If I don't do anything wrong, I won't get yelled at." In a workplace where the only feedback is negative, staff become so worried about avoiding criticism that they stop thinking about anything else.

As destructive as negative feedback can be, there is another type of feedback that is even worse—no feedback at all. The boss doesn't even care enough to yell at me. It doesn't matter what I do, no one notices. While positive feedback leads to commitment to doing the job well and negative feedback to compliance to minimum standards, no feedback leads to employees ignoring job expectations and only doing whatever they feel like doing.

Ask on Behalf of Others

In a busy workplace with lots of employees, many of whom work with minimal direct supervision, it is often difficult for the supervisor to be aware of each employee's contributions. When you are aware of a performance deserving of recognition, ask on another's behalf:

- **As a supervisor, you can let your boss know:**
  "I think the people in my department did a great job on this project. I am sure they would appreciate a few words of acknowledgement for their contributions from you."
- **You can ask your supervisor on behalf of a co-worker:**
  "Joe worked hard to get the month-end report done on time. He came in on the weekend when no one else was here to gather all the necessary information. I think he deserves to be recognized for all this extra work."
- **As a supervisor you can also point out to a staff member when peer recognition would be fitting:**
  "You may not even know this, but Susan was the one who discovered that we were running short of the P12 forms and quietly ordered more without anyone telling her to do that. If she hadn't done that, all of us would have had difficulty completing orders for our clients. You may want to let her know that you appreciated what she did."

Lesson #4: You can't motivate staff with the same old recognition tricks.

Most staff recognition techniques have a short shelf life. An employee may be thrilled the first time she receives a thank-you card from the boss. The next couple are great. And the next few that follow them are seen as "a nice gesture." But when the only way appreciation is expressed is with a thank-you card, the value of this gesture is diminished. How many thank-you cards does a person need?

Using the same recognition technique over and over reduces its effectiveness. To maintain the impact of recognition, supervisors need to vary how they recognize staff. A thank-you

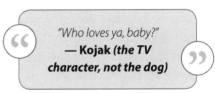

"Who loves ya, baby?"
— **Kojak (the TV character, not the dog)**

card this time, a small gift the next. Maybe a few words on a sticky note or the opportunity to take an extended lunch break. When it comes to effective staff recognition, variety is the spice of life.

One Final Lesson from the World of Dogs and Dog Owners

Dog owners are like grandparents, without the photo albums. When they gather, dog owners talk about their pets. They brag about how cute and intelligent their canine companions are. They describe how obedient and affectionate their dogs are.

"Look at the new trick I taught my dog."

"I found a test of dog IQ in a book. When I tested Rover, he did really well on all 12 tests. He is so smart!"

"I think my dog can tell time. She always knows when my husband is due home from work."

Suppose dogs had similar discussions about people when they meet. Having sniffed each other in places I won't mention here, the conversation would soon turn to their owners.

"They only feed me table scraps," a sad-faced basset hound complains.

"Mine serves me only canned dog food and imported cheese," an uppity poodle says.

"Wow," the Dalmatian exclaims. "Your owner sure treats you well."

Then a cocker spaniel shifts the topic with his inquiry: "What type of treats do they give you?"

I worried how Kojak might respond to this question. Would he regale others with memories of a variety of treats…or complain that that no matter what he does, it is always the "same old, same old?"

Wanting to avoid being known throughout the dog world as the owner who gives boring treats, I decided to enhance my reputation by purchasing a variety of treats. Price was not a consideration as I searched for variety and treat quality. My dog would get more than those bone-shaped cookies that I had been purchasing in five-kg buckets.

I bought packages of special treats to take on our walks. The label on one said they were "100 per cent meat." A dog would love those! Another box contained cookies shaped like cats and mailmen, that tasted like peanut butter—something about which I was content to take the manufacturer's word. With these treats in my pocket, I was confident that Kojak would excitedly do whatever I asked of him.

It did not work that way. Sometimes, he would take one of the premium treats when offered. Other times he would take it, and then after a moment, let it fall to the ground. Or he would simply sniff at it and turn away. On the other hand, whenever he was offered what I perceived to be common treats—the inexpensive bone-shaped one, he accepted them and crunched away happily.

This final lesson had been an expensive one:

Lesson #5: The value of rewards and recognition is determined by the recipient, not the giver.

A whole industry has grown up across North America supplying staff recognition merchandise. I regularly receive catalogues filled with trinkets that the suppliers claim will make it easier for supervisors to recognize staff—certificates, pins, plaques, trophies, T-shirts, jackets, travel mugs and so on.

Just as my money was wasted on expensive dog treats, most of what is spent on staff recognition trinkets is wasted. What it purchases misses the mark. For every person who values and displays a certificate she receives, there is another for whom the certificate has little value. It will never be displayed. After lying around for a few years, the certificate becomes the victim of an aggressive spring cleanup. Other certificates will hit the recycling bin within hours of being received.

When it becomes time for the person who proudly displays her certificate to recognize others, she will be inclined to express appreciation in the way she values—more certificates. Just because a supervisor values certificates—or plaques, trophies, or caps—does not mean her staff will feel the same way. Before purchasing a lifetime supply of certificates, be sure that your staff values them as much as you do. Chances are they won't.

DIY RECOGNITION RESEARCH:
When the Boss Said, "Well done!"

What you will need for this research project:
A pen and paper

Research Process:
1. List at least five times in the past year when your boss acknowledged you for doing your job well.

2. Ask yourself:
   - Were there other times when you did something well and your boss knew about what you did, but didn't say anything?
   - Do you feel that you are getting enough recognition for your contributions to the organization's success? Or do you feel that you receive too much **Genuine** praise and recognition?

Implications for the Workplace:
Were you able to come up with five examples of having been recognized in the last year? How do you think your staff would respond to this question? Would your staff be able to list five times when they received recognition from you?

*Hint: There is always room for more recognition. No one ever feels they are receiving too much **Genuine** recognition.*

Chapter 9
Once is Never Enough

For about 10 years, I worked with university students who were enrolled in a practicum that would lead to them becoming teachers. During one of our classes, I delivered a simple message to the group of aspiring teachers: praise students regularly when they meet expectations. To reinforce this message, I quoted a comment from a student attitude survey that I imagined was written by a boy in Grade Six.

> *"I am a good kid. I always do what the teacher asks. I am never late for class. I always do my homework. I never fool around in class. But in the three years, I have only gotten one Golden Apple."*

I explained that a Golden Apple was a coupon that teachers awarded to students with whose performance they were pleased—a type of instant recognition for being "caught doing good." Every time a teacher awarded a Golden Apple, the student's name was entered for a prize draw at the school's monthly assembly. There was no limit to the number of awards the teacher could give, or the number that an individual student could receive. Many students were multi-award recipients each month.

"Constant kindness can accomplish much. As the sun makes ice melt, kindness causes misunderstanding, mistrust, and hostility to evaporate."
— Albert Schweitzer, *Nobel laureate*

I was describing this program when some of the student teachers noticed that one of their colleagues was crying.

"What's wrong?" one asked, moving to comfort her classmate.

"That student was me," she said. She continued by describing how she, like the student who I had quoted, had always done what was expected of her when she was in school, but no one ever seemed to notice. All around her, other students were receiving awards. Top performers were being recognized as honour students or athletes-of-the-month. Others were described as, "most improved." Some were publicly acknowledged for completing their homework for the first time in weeks, or for not misbehaving for a whole day. The recognition this future teacher had received as a student had been almost non-existent.

She had just made an abstract concept concrete. People, whether elementary school students or adults, need to be acknowledged regularly. No—make that frequently. When recognition is frequent, people feel reassured that they are valued and their contributions appreciated. Frequent recognition builds trust, teamwork, engagement and relationships.

Frequent recognition leads to a culture of recognition. There are workplaces where recognition occurs naturally. Recognition is part of the fabric of the organization—part of everyday life, not a ritual reserved for special occasions. Supervisors and co-workers, alike, acknowledge others

"Great recognition, like any great relationship, requires constant attention and continuous feedback."
— Dee Hansford,
recognition consultant

for their contributions. Recognition-rich work environments are places where people want to be and where they want to contribute.

In work environments where recognition is frequent, staff members are better able to give and receive recognition. By contrast, those working in an environment characterized by infrequent recognition are unsure how to respond when they are recognized. Being recognized makes them suspicious. They anticipate that recognition is the prelude to bad news. When recognition does occur in such an environment, it is seldom seen as **Genuine.**

So, if recognition is best if it is frequent, what does that mean? How often is often enough?

Certainly, frequent is not the right term to describe being invited to a service awards event once every five years. Nor is it frequent recognition if a supervisor saves up a year's worth of recognition and then dumps it on an employee during an annual performance review meeting.

Hopefully, no teacher or supervisor consciously withholds recognition, but sometimes we assume that people don't need as much as they do—the intrinsic reward of a job well done is all people need, we think. While being able to appreciate yourself for what you do is important, the truth is that most individuals desire to experience words and actions of affirmation from others.

Research by The Gallup Organization identified 12 survey questions that, when answered in the affirmative, are indicative of a successful organization (defined as having high productivity, profitability and customer satisfaction and low staff turnover). One of the 12 Gallup questions–"In the last seven days, have I received recognition or praise for good work?"–points to the importance of frequent recognition. With frequency, recognition has a stronger impact on staff morale and motivation. Frequency keeps the feeling of being appreciated, fresh.

"In the most innovative companies, there is a significantly higher volume of thank-yous than in companies of low innovation."
— Rosabeth Moss Kanter,
professor, Harvard Business School

Do We Ever Say We Love Them?

A married couple was sitting in the living room one evening, when the wife spoke to her husband.

"You never say you love me."

Her husband put down his newspaper and looked toward his wife.

"I told you I loved you on the day when we were married 30 years ago. If that changes, I'll be sure to let you know."

It's an old joke, but it raises the question: how often do we tell staff members we love them?

We do when we hire them. We enthusiastically welcome them and say we are glad they have come to work for us.

And then, what? Too often, just silence.

A business case can definitely be made for more staff recognition. Gallup found that people who don't feel appreciated are less engaged, which can reduce productivity and profitability by 10 to 20 per cent. When employees feel they are inadequately recognized, they are twice as likely to say they plan to quit. Another study found that about 70 per cent of top performers who received regular feedback were likely to stay, while only about 40 per cent who did not receive feedback felt the same loyalty to their employer.

Workers of all ages require regular, positive feedback. This appears to be particularly true for younger workers, frequently referred to as generation X (born between 1965 and 1980) and millennials (born after 1980). Researchers report that younger workers want to know how they are doing…

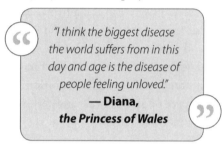

"I think the biggest disease the world suffers from in this day and age is the disease of people feeling unloved."
— **Diana, the Princess of Wales**

now! In addition to being immediate, this feedback needs to be **Relevant** so that they know they are on track. The feedback also needs to be **Explicit** and **Genuine.** Generation Xers can spot praise that is being given just for the sake of giving praise.

Meeting the needs of generation X and millennials is important, but this doesn't mean that the recognition needs of boomers (born between 1946 and 1965) can be ignored. It may have been too long since someone was last recognized.

The Shipping News, the 1994 Pulitzer Prize-winning novel by Annie Proulx, follows the adventures and misadventures of Quoyle, a boomer who becomes a reporter for *Gammy Bird,* a weekly newspaper serving communities along the Newfoundland coast. At one point in the story, Quoyle is called into his editor's office. There he is told that people liked a story he wrote about a ship that was visiting the harbour. The boss asks him to produce a similar column each week.

He returns to his desk where we will have Ms. Proulx pick up the narrative: "Quoyle rolled paper into the typewriter but didn't type anything. Thirty-six years old and this was the first time anybody ever said he'd done it right."

How many 36-year-old employees are still waiting to hear someone say that they are doing their jobs right?

At Least 2 Ways to Ensure Recognition is Frequent

1. Begin your week by listing all your staff members on your to-do list. Set a goal of being able to check off every name before the end of the week, after having recognized that individual in some way for having done the job well.

2. Place each staff member's name on the top of an index card. Each time you recognize that individual, record the date and why the person was recognized. Thumb through the cards regularly. If you discover that you have not acknowledged someone in some way for more than two weeks, commit to finding a reason to do so within the next 24 hours.

"To keep a lamp burning, we have to keep putting oil in it."
— Mother Teresa

DIY RECOGNITION RESEARCH:
Feeling Good About Work

What you will need for this research project:
You; a few friends, family members or colleagues; pen and paper

Research Process:
1. Recall and list five times when you felt particularly good about your work.
2. Put a checkmark next to each of those occasions when your memory is the result of receiving feedback from a supervisor, co-worker or customer?
3. Repeat steps 1 and 2 with one or more friends or colleagues.

Implications for the Workplace:
How many of these best workplace memories included times when you received negative feedback—you were told you could do your job better?

How many of these best workplace memories included times when you received positive feedback or recognition?

How many of these involved formal recognition events or programs? Informal recognition?

Hint: Many of us remember times when we received negative feedback, but we likely would not include these in our lists of favourite on-the-job memories.

Chapter 10
Money Don't Buy You Much These Days... and Likely Never Could

A graffiti artist's message on a mailbox near our home must have confused some passers-bys.

"I spent my $400 on spray paint."

The reference was to the one-time "prosperity dividend" paid by the Alberta government to every resident of the province in 2005.

Confusion is understandable among those who did not live in the province at the time and didn't receive a cheque. But not so with those who did live in Alberta. Surely they would remember receiving $400 tax-free...and how they spent it.

Wrong!

Over past few years, I have been asking people attending my presentations who were living in Alberta in 2005 if they remember receiving the cheques. Some do. Many don't.

And how did they spend the money?

"Not sure."

"Paid bills, I guess."

"Must have spent it on something. Nothing special."

"Compensation is a right; recognition is a gift."
— **Rosabeth Moss Kanter, *professor, Harvard Business School***

They are like most employees who receive bonuses. They don't remember how much they received, why they received it, or how they spent it. The money doesn't stay long in the employees' pockets—or in their memories.

It's like the birthday money we received from our great-aunts when we were children. We intended to spend it on "something special," as the elderly relative requested in the note that was enclosed with the cash. What we did spend it on was…well, we don't actually remember. All we remember is that a few days later, the money was gone and we had nothing to show for it. It was quickly gone, and nearly as soon, forgotten.

Money doesn't work as a means of recognizing staff, because it doesn't last. It has no "trophy value." It produces nothing we can point to later or brag about. A cheque is a cheque. It just arrives. There is none of the intangible reward associated with the boss taking time to thank you with a pat on the back. It was there, and now it's gone. And we don't know where it went.

A study by American Express Incentive Services found that about 30 per cent of employees who had received a bonus had used the money to pay bills. Not a bad thing to do, but hardly something to brag about.

The next most frequent response when asked how they spent their bonus? About 20 per cent replied that they could not remember what they had done with the money. Certainly nothing to brag about there!

Next were the 10 per cent who couldn't even remember receiving the bonus. Further down the list were those who recalled using the money to buy something for a family member, add to their savings, or buy something special for themselves.

The practice of rewarding employees with cash payments can have unexpected consequences, most of which aren't good. A few years ago, an Australian who was part of a group I was with, touring Scandinavia and Russia, told me that his sister had recently received a $25,000 bonus from the IT company for which she worked.

"Except for the financially desperate, people do not work for money alone. What also fuels their passion for work is a larger sense of purpose or passion. Given the opportunity, people gravitate to what gives them meaning, to what engages to the fullest their commitment, talent, energy, and skill. And that can be changing jobs to get a better fit with what matters to us."
— Daniel Goleman, *Working with Emotional Intelligence*

"That sounds great," I responded. "She must feel really good about where she works."

"Not really. She's looking for another job."

"Why? They just gave her an extra $25,000."

"She feels unappreciated. The year before she received $50,000."

Likely, she worked for a company that paid bonuses based on the company's performance. The better the company does, the bigger the bonus employees receive.

Logically, this makes good sense. Companies base bonuses on measures that are **Relevant** to what the company says is important. They define the criteria that will be used to determine the size of the bonuses, such as productivity, profitability, safety performance, staff turnover levels and absenteeism. The better the results for these measures, the bigger the bonus. If the right numbers are up and the wrong numbers are down, the cash bonus is bigger. When the right numbers are down and the wrong numbers are up, the bonus is smaller, or not paid at all.

Yes, it makes good sense, unless people have come to depend on receiving a big bonus each year. There may have been a time when staff anticipated how they would spend their bonus if they received one. Today it seems that people spend in anticipation of receiving a bonus. What might once have been a way to express appreciation for results achieved has become something people have come to depend on receiving. What once was a reward for doing a good job had become an entitlement—just another part of the compensation package.

A woman once told me how upset her husband and his co-workers were with their employer after three years of declining bonuses, from thousands of dollars to just a few hundred. "They count on that money. They expect to get it, so they make commitments and buy things on their credit cards, planning to pay it off when their bonuses arrive."

"And often, rewards tied to organizational performance do not feel very relevant or motivating to employees, because they simply do not see tight links between their effort and the rewarded results. The rewards don't seem to be very controllable to them."
— Alexander Hiam, *Motivational Management*

While productivity, profitability, safety performance, staff turnover levels and absenteeism are all valid indicators of the organization's success, typically there is little that most individuals can do to influence the numbers. Those who do have direct impact on the numbers may be tempted to take actions that will affect the bonus criteria positively in the short term, but may have long-term negative effects on the company: delaying expensive equipment repair or upgrades, under-reporting injuries, ignoring safety violations or misreporting profits and loses.

Prior to the recession of 2008, some employers found it difficult to retain staff. One solution was to offer significant cash retention bonuses, paid to people who stayed with the company for a specified period. In some cases, the program backfired as employees held off submitting their resignations just until the bonus cash was safely in their bank accounts.

Cash rewards are seldom **Timely.** It's not like the boss is going to open his wallet and hand an individual a few bills as soon as he see behaviour that deserves recognition. Someone has to recommend payment of a bonus, someone else needs to authorize its payment and finally, someone has to process the cheque. By the time the money arrives, the circumstances that prompted the payment are only a vague memory.

When everyone is rewarded with similar bonuses, no one feels that she was singled out for recognition because of her contribution. When everyone is rewarded in the same way, no one feels rewarded.

How companies pay bonuses varies. Sometimes payments come as separate cheques to distinguish the bonus from regular compensation. Unfortunately, the distinction between wages and a bonus doesn't matter at tax time. To the taxman, both are seen as income. Both are taxable. It is another unanticipated outcome of using cash to recognize staff.

By tax time, most employees will have forgotten receiving the money or why they received it. The immediate gratification of the bonus has long passed. All that is left is the pain of having to pay taxes on the extra money.

"You can't buy people's time; you can buy their physical presence at a given time; you can even buy a measured number of their muscular motions per hour. But you cannot buy enthusiasm…you cannot buy loyalty…you cannot buy the devotion of their hearts. You must earn these."
— **Martin Luther King, Jr.**

> ## Just Like Cash
>
> Gifts are out and gift cards are in. Organizations see gift cards as a convenient alternative to merchandise when recognizing service awards, retirements and the contributions and achievements of staff members. The use of gift cards saves time and eliminates the need to maintain an inventory of recognition gifts.
>
> It is also easier to please recipients. With the variety of gift cards to select from, it is easy to personalize recognition, providing each recipient with the opportunity to choose his "gift"—be it dinner a favourite restaurant, travel and recreation, or something from a preferred retailer.
>
> But anyone who uses gift cards when recognizing staff should understand there is a downside to their use. The Canada Revenue Agency views gift cards as "near cash," which makes them taxable as income, even if used in situations where employer gifts with a value of up to $500 would be not be seen as taxable. In its *2009 Employer's Guide, Taxable Benefits and Allowances,* the CRA states that, "Cash and near-cash gifts or awards are always a taxable benefit to the employee . . .We consider the gift card or gift certificate to be a taxable benefit to the employee because there is an element of choice."
>
> For more on this topic, see www.GREATstaffrecogntion.com/articles/taxes.

Wages and benefits are what get new staff in the door, but it's not what causes them to stay. If it was, the company that won the bidding war would have all the employees it needed—until someone else bids higher. But that's not the way things work. Money doesn't buy loyalty. To get people to stay, a workplace must offer more than just money.

"Money has never made man happy, nor will it; there is nothing in its nature to produce happiness. The more of it one has the more one wants."
— **Ben Franklin, *American statesman***

At Least 8 Ways Cash Can Become
A Useful Recognition Tool

For some staff members and under certain circumstances, cash may be an **Appropriate** staff recognition tool to use when acknowledging the contributions of an individual:

1. Cash would likely mean most to someone in a low-wage job, just beginning his career, or facing unexpected bills.
2. A coin collector may welcome something to add to his collection.
3. Paycheques or pay notifications could be delivered personally, along with specific examples of how the individual contributed over the pay period.
4. Just before a staff member leaves for vacation, she could be presented with a small amount of foreign currency that she can use during her travels.
5. While not real cash, a few foil-wrapped chocolate coins are a fun way to convey a message of appreciation.
6. Staff members could be sent to the mall with a specific amount of cash with instructions to purchase something for themselves within a specific time period.
7. A donation could be made to a charity selected by the staff member—not the manager.
8. When a staff member offers a great suggestion, present her with a shinny new penny, with a message that her "thought was worth much more than a penny!"

"But too many organizations are trying to manage by what we call 'bread alone.' They offer above-average pay and benefits, the 'bread,' if you will, and expect that to make up for the significant shortcomings in their work environments. But today's worker will not stay at a job—and certainly will not stay committed to a job (even a good-paying, prestigious one)—if she's not satisfied."
— Adrian Gostick and Chester Elton,
Managing with Carrots

DIY RECOGNITION RESEARCH:
Do They Remember Where the Cash Went?

What you will need for this research project:
A few employees of an organization that provides cash incentives for a job well done

Research Process:
1. Ask, "When is the last time you received a cash award for a job well done? What had you done to receive this award?"
2. Listen to the response. Particularly note responses such as, "I dunno," or "Everyone got them," or "I guess they were happy with my work."
3. Ask, "How did you spend this money?"
4. Record the responses:

Possible Responses	Number of Responses
Paid some bills	
Bought something special for myself	
Bought something special for family member(s)	
Can't remember how I spent it	
Bought lottery tickets	
Can't remember receiving any money	
Saved or invested it	
Used for other purposes	

Implications for the Workplace:
What is the lasting effect of cash rewards? Do employees remember them or understand why they received them? Has the cash reward become an entitlement that they depend upon to support their lifestyle? Is the cash just an extension of their paycheque?

Hint: The problem with cash is that it has no staying power. It is received, then spent. Incentives and bonuses initially introduced to reward or motivate soon become entitlements that employees depend on receiving.

Please note that this form is available online at:
www.GREATstaffrecognition.com/bookbonus/DIYforms
You have permission to print it for your use to conduct this recognition research.

Chapter 11
Never Send 'Em Lunch!

I had gone to a prospective client's office to meet him for a lunch meeting. We were about to leave when he stopped to speak to his secretary.

"Did you arrange to have lunch sent to the guys in the maintenance department?"

Assured that lunch would be delivered as scheduled, he turned to me. "We can go now."

Curious about what I had just witnessed, I waited until we had ordered before asking, "What was that about?"

"This is our Maintenance Staff Appreciation Week. Staff in other departments are encouraged to do something for members of the maintenance team all this week to show them they are appreciated," he explained. "I decided that our department would send them lunch."

We went on to discuss other topics, but I couldn't get the image of the maintenance staff gathering for lunch from my mind. Eventually, I realized what was wrong with this picture. The manager across from me had selected the wrong lunch companion. Instead of enjoying lunch in an upscale restaurant, he should have been in the maintenance department lunchroom, sharing pizza or Chinese food with the men and women who worked there.

"The only gift is a portion of thyself."
— Ralph Waldo Emerson, *American essayist and poet*

While I imagine that the maintenance staff appreciated the lunch, I felt that one ingredient was missing—the manager across from me. Having lunch delivered to the maintenance staff was a nice gesture, but the message that they are valued would have resonated much more strongly if the manager had taken them lunch and then stayed to share it with them.

In his absence, it was just free food. A week later, chances are that the staff won't remember–or care–whether they ate pizza or Chinese. What they could have remembered is how they felt when a manager from another department took the time to bring them lunch and stay to eat with them. The most valuable gift any of us can give to others is our time. When the manager is present, the focus shifts from the food to the employees. They are worth more than the cost of some food from a take-out restaurant.

If you are a supervisor, you are one of the most important people in your staff's work life. You may have hired them and you could fire them. You are the one who assigns their work. Every action you take is analyzed. Everything you say and do helps to shape the quality of the staff member's work experience. The time you spend—or don't spend—with employees sends powerful messages. Are they valued enough for you to spend time with them?

When I worked in the school system, one of my responsibilities was to recruit and select people to take on leadership roles in schools—principals and vice principals. One of

"Kids spell love T-I-M-E."
— John Crudele, speaker and author

the tools available to me was a standardized interview protocol that I was trained to use. Now, more than a decade after I last used this instrument, I recall few of its 70 questions, but there is one that I will remember forever:

"Do you want your staff to like you?"

Typically, the would-be school administrators would respond that being liked was less important than being respected by their staff. This answer may have captured the conventional wisdom, but it was wrong. Being liked by your staff is important. The research upon which the interview questions were based concluded that employees were likely to work harder for a supervisor who they liked.

This didn't mean that respect was unimportant. It is important, and it is not automatic. It must be earned. People may respect the position, but they are unlikely to like or respect a person who occupies the position who they never see or get to know.

Respect only comes to those managers who employees know, like and trust. These perceptions are based on how employees are treated and how they feel the boss feels about them. Supervisors who demonstrate their respect for their staff are more likely to earn respect from staff.

Employees won't like someone because he buys them lunch, but they may come to like and respect someone who spends time with them, talks with them, asks questions and listens. If this person also brings lunch, that is a bonus.

While food is always a good starting point, visits with staff don't always need to include lunch. Take along a box of doughnuts or muffins, or a few cups of coffee. Just drop in for no purpose, other than to chat. If yours is a 24/7 operation, this may mean visiting the worksite at 3:00 a.m.

One of my former bosses would occasionally spend evenings dropping into schools to visit with the night custodians. They loved it. He listened to what they were saying and they respected him for that.

Sometimes, you may invite a group of staff members to join you for a meal at a local restaurant. When you do, remember that this type of recognition is about them, not you. Consider food restrictions and dining preferences. Some may be vegetarians, have food allergies or be on restricted diets due to religious beliefs or medical conditions. Just because it is your favourite food doesn't mean it will be **Appropriate** for them.

"Listening makes people feel understood and supported, which in turn helps them do better work. In addition, good listening skills strengthen relationships between managers and employees by creating mutual respect."
— **Ken Blanchard, "Communication Skills Crucial for the '90s," Quality Digest, April 1991**

The Phantom Coffee Elf

It is a tale reminiscent of the Shoemaker and the Elves by the Brothers Grimm. When no one was around, several steaming cups of coffee from a nearby coffee shop mysteriously appeared on the staff room table.

The staff members were perplexed. Where had the coffee come from? To whom did the coffee belong? Why was it here? Was it for them? Should they help themselves?

This same scene played itself out several times. Eventually the staff discovered the source—a senior executive—and that the coffee was intended for them. What they never understood was why the coffee appeared, other than a vague sense that it was meant as an expression of appreciation.

The executive offered no explanation. After each delivery, he would disappear into his office. He never remained to hand the cups of coffee to staff members, to explain why he was expressing appreciation in this fashion or to join the conversation around the staff room table.

His absence robbed what could have been a powerful act of appreciation of its impact.

As part of the celebrations of a mining company's 25th anniversary, the CEO invited employees who had been with the company since the beginning to his home for a gourmet dinner with fine wine. For some, it was a great experience, but for others...well, let's say it would have been better had the CEO invited them over for a few beers and steaks on the barbeque.

I had a similar misadventure when I was a school principal. Wishing to show my appreciation to our custodians, I invited them to join me for lunch at my favourite restaurant. It wasn't one of my best moments in staff recognition. My guests seemed uncomfortable in this unfamiliar environment. One struggled to read the menu. Another confessed that she seldom ate lunch. The conversation was stilted at times, and non-existent at others.

It turned out to be a great learning experience. The next time I wanted to say thank you to the custodians, I picked up a couple of pizzas and a few soft drinks, and met them in a familiar setting: the school's staff room. The conversation flowed and I left with a greater appreciation for who they were as individuals, and a better understanding and more respect for the work they did.

During these informal visits, the manager's role is to speak little and listen a lot. In this way, these visits are similar to an interview. Because you want to learn as much about the prospective employee in a limited amount of time, you want to encourage the candidate to do most of the talking (during my *Interview Right to Hire Right* workshops I suggest an 80/20 ratio, with the candidate talking at least 80 per cent of the time).

As when interviewing, you should come prepared with a mental list of work-related questions to stimulate the discussion, if necessary:

- How is the job going?
- What problems have you encountered? How were you able to solve them?
- What's been going well? Why do you feel this has been the case?
- Which part of the work makes you feel particularly proud?
- If you were running things around here, what one thing could we do to serve customers better (or improve productivity, or cut costs)?

You will find that in these conversations–as during job interviews–people like to talk about what they do well.

Conversations with existing staff differ from hiring interviews in one significant way: it doesn't matter who controls the agenda. During interviews, managers must be ever vigilant against candidates who will skilfully shift the conversation to topics that show them in a good light and reflect well on their knowledge and experience. On the other hand, the interviewer wants to cover the same territory with all candidates to establish common ground upon which to compare and select whom to hire.

During informal workplace conversations, it not only doesn't matter who controls the agenda, it may even be better if staff members dictate what will be discussed. Once it is clear that staff members wish to discuss a particular topic, the manager should be quick to abandon his agenda—you can always return to your agenda later or during future conversations.

Allowing staff to decide what will be discussed shows that you, the supervisor, feel that what they have to say is important enough to be listened to. By listening, you will discover what is important to them and may gain insight into them as individuals. They may move to more

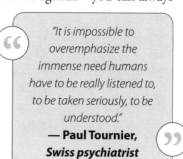

"It is impossible to overemphasize the immense need humans have to be really listened to, to be taken seriously, to be understood."
— **Paul Tournier,**
Swiss psychiatrist

personal topics, such as family, non-work-related interests, hobbies and career goals. Through these conversations, you can come to know your staff as individuals. This knowledge can offer clues that will enable you to provide more **Appropriate** recognition in the future.

Whether the conversation is directed by your questions or by what staff members have on their minds, your response should be the same. Listen attentively. Ask questions to clarify or to delve deeper into what they are saying. Take notes. When necessary, offer to get back to them with answers to their questions. Keep these commitments.

Frequently during informal conversations, you will hear a gem of an idea that if implemented will benefit your organization—ideas on how to serve customers better, improve product or service quality, increase productivity or reduce costs.

When this happens, let staff know how you will be able to use the information they gave you. If possible, involve the person making the suggestion in preparing for its implementation. Tell others the source of the innovation. Give credit to the person responsible for the innovation.

Much can come as the result of sitting down over lunch or coffee to talk with—and especially to listen to—one person or a group of staff members. But these opportunities are lost forever if you just send 'em lunch!

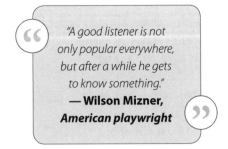

"A good listener is not only popular everywhere, but after a while he gets to know something."
— **Wilson Mizner,**
American playwright

At Least 7 Ways to Use Food to Show
Team Members They Are Appreciated

1. Take them lunch and stay to share the meal with them. Ask them about their work, especially what they do well. Listen to their ideas.
2. Purchase cups of gourmet coffee and personally deliver it to their workstations. Meet them in the staff room for a pot of coffee and offer to pour.
3. On a hot summer day, deliver ice cream to their workstations.
4. Greet staff at the door with a steaming cup of hot chocolate on a dark, cold winter morning.
5. Bake cookies or muffins and serve them to staff during the morning coffee break.
6. At a busy time when staff has been working to the max, cook up breakfast for them one morning, or have a barbeque lunch to show them you appreciate how hard they have been working. Note: It is not a good idea to hold a potluck lunch during a busy time. Your staff does not need an extra work-related task.
7. Invite a staff member to join you for lunch. Allow him to suggest a convenient time and select the restaurant. You may even ask him to invite a co-worker to join you.

"If employees are upset and don't feel cared for, what will be first in their minds is their resume, not the customer."
— Hal Rosenbluth,
American businessman
and author

DIY RECOGNITION RESEARCH:
Where Did All the Employees-of-the-Month Go?

What you will need for this research project:
An organization that has space to display photos and/or names of its employee-of-the-month, but where there are no photos; even more chutzpah than was required for the earlier employee-of-the-month research project (see page 32).

Research Process:
1. Visit an organization that has not changed its employee-of-the-month display in months—there is no photo or the photo is for January's Employee of the Month, and it's already June. If there is a list of employees-of-the-month, the list ended three months ago.
2. Seek out the manager. Ask, "Does the absence of a current photo or names for the last three months mean that nobody does his or her job well enough to deserve to be named as the employee-of-the-month?"
3. Listen to the response. Particularly note responses such as, "We haven't got around to picking an employee-of-the-month," or "We've just been too busy that we haven't had time to take a photo or add names to the employee-of-the-month plaque."
4. Ask, "What else do you do to recognize staff for their contributions?"
5. Listen to the response. Don't be surprised by vague descriptions of effort to recognize staff or a more direct, "Nothing in particular."
6. Leave quickly and quietly if asked to do so by security.

Supplementary question (for extra credit):
"How much time do you spend hiring new staff to replace those who leave because they feel unappreciated?"

Implications for the Workplace:
Is it difficult to find time to recognize staff? What message does that send to staff about how much they are valued? If you don't have time to let staff know they are appreciated, where do you find time to recruit, hire and train replacements?

Hint: Staff recognition programs become stale. People lose interest. When supervisors and managers depend on programs to do the job, the amount of recognition employees get is too infrequent to be effective.

Chapter 12
In the Words of Others

It's evening. The men of a Punjabi village in India gather for conversation, during which much of the focus will be on community members who are not present, a practice known locally as "gupshup."

Such idle talk is not unique to Punjabi culture. In fact, discussion of other people–their actions and motivations–is common throughout the world. Researchers suggest that 60 per cent of all conversations are about people who are not present.

In other words, we gossip a lot. It is the stuff of popular magazines, radio and TV talk shows, and workplace chit-chat.

Gossip gets a bad rap. We think of it as focused on the personal and private lives of others, usually in a malicious way. It turns out that that's really not the case. Most gossip is actually benign, and frequently positive. It also serves a cultural purpose. Gossip is one of the oldest and most common ways to share information. It contributes to our understanding of the world, our community and the workplace. Participants in these conversations can learn about cultural norms and what the speaker regards as important, through his comments about behaviour that is proper or improper.

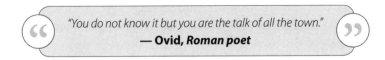

"You do not know it but you are the talk of all the town."
— **Ovid, Roman poet**

The implications for staff recognition relates, of course, to positive comments about absent co-workers:

"Abbas did a wonderful job of sorting out the problem Mrs. Stephens had with the delivery of her new furniture."

"When I dropped by Jane's classroom yesterday, she was teaching an interesting lesson on the fall of the Roman Empire."

"We had a very upset mother in the ER yesterday. Her baby was vomiting and had a high temperature. Jennifer was very good with her. She listened to her concerns, answered her questions and reassured her that her baby would receive great care."

Each of these examples is typical of what is said about people who aren't present. While the people who made these observations about Abbas, Jane and Jennifer should have made them to those they are now praising, they likely have not. Having heard the comments, you can make up for these failures to praise.

"I was talking to the vice principal yesterday, and she was telling me about a lesson on the fall of the Roman Empire which she saw you teach. She seemed quite impressed by what she saw. She said the students seemed very interested in what you were teaching and seemed to understand what caused Rome's decline."

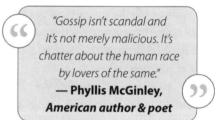

"Gossip isn't scandal and it's not merely malicious. It's chatter about the human race by lovers of the same."
— **Phyllis McGinley, American author & poet**

Even if the person who observed the lesson may have already shared her thoughts with Jane, Jane won't suffer from hearing these comments a second time. There is also something special about second-hand praise. When positive comments are repeated they can seem more **Genuine,** as they are spoken without any expectation that they would be passed on.

Such unsolicited, healthy gossip is not the only way to gather positive comments about staff members. Organizations have introduced techniques to encourage customers to provide positive feedback.

Many companies encourage customers to complete comment cards. These may produce positive comments about staff, although many of them are worded in ways that invite more complaints than commendations. They ask

How's My Driving?

How often have you come up behind a company vehicle—usually a company truck—bearing a sign that reads:

"How's my driving? Phone 1-8**-I-TATTLE."

"If this vehicle is not being driven in a courteous manner, call 1-555-RAT-FINK."

Says a lot about the atmosphere of trust that exists within these companies, doesn't it?

customers to tell them about what went wrong or how the company could do better. Doubtless, the resulting information will be useful as the company strives to improve service, but the responses provide little positive feedback to be shared with staff.

There are exceptions. Holiday Inn Hotels invites guests to nominate staff members for its Shining Stars Employee Recognition Program. "If one of our employees has made a difference for you, please fill out this form and give it to any Guest Service Representative." The Real Canadian Superstore makes ABCD cards available that ask shoppers, "What actions did you observe that are Above and Beyond the Call of Duty?" On the final day at sea on Princess Cruises, *You Make The Difference!* cards appear around the ship. "If any of our crew members have gone the 'extra mile' to make your cruise extra special, we would like to know in order to thank them for a job well done, to enter their names into the 'Employee of the Month Program' and to place your Service Recognition Nomination in their personnel file to promote career growth."

Collecting customer comments, alone, will not do anything positive unless they are shared with the staff members in a **Timely** fashion. In some cases, the customer comments are used to select a limited number of employees for corporate awards. The award winners may hear the positive feedback—although sometime they aren't shared and winners are unsure why they won—but the others (i.e. losers) never hear or read the customers' words. Comments about non-winners are simply discarded.

Other organizations place the comments in the employees' personnel files, perhaps to be shared during some future performance appraisal.

"The only time people dislike gossip is when you gossip about them."
— **Will Rogers, *American humourist***
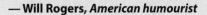

The superintendent of a school district for whom we conducted attitude surveys for several years understood the value of ensuring that every staff member about whom a positive comment was made received this praise. She asked us to include a question on student surveys that asked students to think about a teacher or other staff member who made a difference in their school career. What made this person special? After the survey results were collected, these comments were sorted and the superintendent sent each teacher, educational assistant, secretary or principal a letter that included the students' comments—along with not-infrequent praise from parents and co-workers collected from other surveys. Some staff members who received one of these letters posted it in the classroom or added it to their professional portfolios.

Costco appears to understand the value of passing on positive comments from customers. In all the stores that I have visited, positive comment cards–often accompanied by a photo of the individual named by the customer–are displayed on a bulletin board near the entrance to the staff break room.

Using the Words of Others to Express Her Thoughts

When she can't think of the right words to express appreciation, an acquaintance of ours reaches for the collection of quotations that she keeps on her desk. There she finds a quotation that captures what she is feeling, which she uses when writing thank-you notes to volunteers or donors.

"If you want your children to improve, let them overhear the nice things you say about them to others."
— **Haim Ginott, *child psychologist***

**At Least 7 Ways to Use the Words
of Others to Recognize Staff**

1. Create a "Wall of Fame" where customer comment cards, letters and newspaper articles can be displayed for both customers and staff to read.
2. Collect letters, comment cards and media stories in a binder that is available in the reception areas for visitors to review while waiting for appointments.
3. Ensure that every time a positive comment or letter is received it is forwarded to the staff member in a **Timely** manner. No positive comment should ever be wasted.
4. Whenever you hear someone make a positive comment about a staff member who is not present, encourage her to repeat her observations to that staff member—in person, via email or in writing.
5. Reinforce the words of others by adding your comments, pointing out how the individual or team's actions were **Relevant** to the organization's mission statement, values or goals.
6. After a staff member has presented a successful training session, collect the positive comments from the evaluations, paste them on a sheet, laminate them and present them to the seminar leader with a few positive comments of your own.
7. Collect testimonials from co-workers and present them to an employee on his employment anniversary.

"There is one thing in the world worse than being talked about, and that is not being talked about."
**— Oscar Wilde,
Irish writer and poet**

Chapter 13
Trust Recognition to Those Who Know Best

In a conversation a few years ago, an elementary school teacher proudly recalled a compliment she had received from a teacher who taught in the classroom next door.

"I really appreciate getting students in my class that you had the year before," the colleague said. "They are so ready to learn and excited about school."

What made this recognition so meaningful to the person receiving it was that it came from someone whose opinion she trusted—a respected colleague. This gave these comments instant credibility.

From listening to participants in my seminars and from reviewing responses to staff attitude surveys we have conducted for clients, I have learned how much workers from a variety of work settings crave recognition. They want someone to notice what they do, and value and appreciate them for their efforts and accomplishments.

The usual response to low satisfaction scores concerning recognition is to focus on those in supervisory roles. What are managers doing to recognize staff? Why aren't they doing more? How could they do a better job of recognizing staff?

While it is appropriate to encourage those who supervise to do more, managers and supervisors should not be seen as the only source of recognition. To do so overlooks a potent source of meaningful staff recognition: co-workers.

Peer Recognition Tools for Staff

A second version of this chapter, rewritten for front-line staff, is available at www.greatstaffrecognition.com/articles/peer. You have my permission to makes copies of that article for your staff as a way of giving them some tools they need to engage in peer recognition.

Recognition by peers may be the most powerful type of recognition there is. Who knows better what an employee does than someone who works beside him and does the same or a similar job? Who is a better judge of results than someone who depends on a co-worker to do her job well so she can do her job well? It's certainly not a manager, who is tucked away in his office or is always being called away to meetings. Peers can recognize co-workers instantly when they see behaviour that contributes to success.

Supervisors see the results of employees' efforts, but co-workers see and understand what is being done to achieve those results. They see their teammates' daily frustrations when things go wrong. They experience similar joys when things go well. Co-workers depend on each other to be successful. When others do their jobs well, it makes it easier for the individual to succeed.

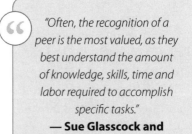

"Often, the recognition of a peer is the most valued, as they best understand the amount of knowledge, skills, time and labor required to accomplish specific tasks."
— **Sue Glasscock and Kimberly Gram, *Workplace Recognition***

When one does the math, peer recognition just makes good sense as a way to provide employees with the recognition they deserve. One supervisor alone can't possibly provide enough recognition.

Picture a manager who is conscientious about recognizing staff. She faithfully takes time every day to recognize at least three staff members—maybe with a thank-you note, a short visit to their worksite, or a small gift given in appreciation of a task done well. This manager even keeps good records to ensure that all staff members are recognized regularly. Sounds like the perfect recognizer, doesn't she?

With 20 people on staff, it would take this manager seven work days to recognize each staff member once, assuming that she recognized three people each day, always waiting until everyone had their "turn" before recognizing a staff member again, no matter how deserving. This also assumes that her plans to recognize staff are never disrupted by meetings or other tasks.

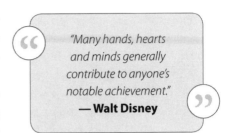

> *"Many hands, hearts and minds generally contribute to anyone's notable achievement."*
> **— Walt Disney**

Given the reality of the workplace—being called away to meetings, reacting to crisis or responding to last minute requests—it would likely take two weeks or longer for even this conscientious recognizer to acknowledge every employee at least once. That's likely not enough. Even those who work for this manager would likely complain that they are not being recognized often enough.

Peer recognition provides employees with an opportunity to stop fretting about the lack of recognition and take matters into their own hands. By doing so, they can significantly increase the recognition everyone receives. Assuming that each person recognizes just one co-worker each week, this would increase the potential that all staff would hear words of appreciation more often.

Co-workers have an advantage as recognizers. The recognition received from co-workers is more easily seen as **Genuine.** Unlike those in supervisory positions, there are no automatic expectations that they will recognize their peers.

Recognition Passed from One to Another

During a break in a customer-service workshop I was presenting to employees of a financial institution about 10 years ago, one participant went to her desk to get something. She returned with a trophy. She proudly explained that she had received it from a co-worker as recognition for something that she had done. She explained that she was now expected to pass the award along to someone else to recognize his or her efforts.

Introducing a similar pass-along award in your workplace is easy to do. The award itself can be practically anything; an old sports trophy, a stuffed toy or a dried flower arrangement. The pass-along award could be themed to the nature of the business—a toy fire truck for firefighters, an apple for educators, a spray-painted gold floppy disk for those working in IT, or a stethoscope for health-care workers. Almost anything will do. What is important is the message of appreciation that the award will help convey.

Having the pass-along award on her desk reminds the recipient of what she accomplished. Its presence on her desk will catch the attentions of co-workers, customers and visitors, who may ask questions that will provide opportunities for the recipient to talk about her success. These conversations may conclude with a discussion about which co-worker deserves to be the next recipient of the pass-along award.

To get started, invite one employee to be first to present the award. Ask him to choose a co-worker who deserves recognition. Explain to everyone that once they receive the pass-along award they should begin to search for a co-worker who deserves to become the next recipient. The award should remain with one recipient for only a short time—never more than a few days, or better still, only a few hours. Staff will soon learn that it is okay to let go of this symbol of their successes, because it will likely return soon.

Enhance Your Pass-along Award

- Attach a plaque to the award with this message: "I am happy to visit but my visit must be brief. Please pass me along to a deserving co-worker."
- Accompany the award with a journal in which the giver explains why she is passing along the award. Not only can the recipient read why he is getting the award, but also why others received recognition previously.

While the award itself is nice to receive, what's really important is to understand what motivated the recognition. Every time the award is presented, the person passing it along should accompany it with a brief note explaining why the recognition is being given. This act of "putting it in writing" could be enhanced with an email to all staff announcing that the award has been passed along, and explaining why.

Recognition During Staff Meetings

Workshop participants say that they regularly devote staff-meeting time to peer recognition. The person leading the meeting invites staff to describe ways in which colleagues has helped them.

At first blush, this would seem to be a positive way to make recognition part of the organization's culture. And this certainly is the case if handled properly, but there is a downside if peer recognition at staff meetings is not done well.

Here are some dos and don'ts to keep in mind when you add peer recognition to your staff meeting:

Do

- Schedule time for peer recognition at the beginning of the meeting, where the most important business should occur.
- Let meeting participants know ahead of time that there will be time devoted to recognition so they can arrive armed with thoughts about which co-workers they will recognize, and why.
- Prime the pump by approaching a few staff members prior to the meeting, to ensure they will come prepared to get the ball rolling when you ask if anyone has someone they would like to recognize. Call upon them first.
- Limit each staff member to recognizing one individual or group at a time so that no one dominates the recognition period.
- Limit the time devoted to recognition during the meeting to avoid exhausting the reasons for recognition, or worse yet, cause meeting participants to fill the available time with contrived or forced recognition.
- Remind staff that recognition is not limited to meeting times. They should express appreciation to co-workers between meetings.
- Provide a template for peer recognition
  - Who is being recognized
  - What he or she did
  - How this behaviour helped the recognizer, the organization or someone else
- Recognize the recognizers. Thank them individually for recognizing their co-workers.
- Begin the first few meetings after you introduce peer recognition by recognizing an individual for something she has done before calling on others to recognize their peers. Eventually, this time should be devoted exclusively to peer recognition. There are other ways and other times when you can recognize staff members.

Don't

- Continue to request recognition until the supply of reasons to recognize dries up.
- Point out who hasn't been recognized so far ("Come on! Can't anyone think of at least one nice thing to say about Albert?")
- Believe that by encouraging staff-meeting recognition that this eliminates the need for other forms of recognition at other times outside meetings.
- Believe that peer recognition eliminates the need for recognition from supervisors.

Give Your Meetings a Recognition Bounce

Set aside a few minutes at staff meetings to toss around a "recognition ball." Get started by inviting those who wish to thank co-workers for their assistance to raise their hands. Throw a soft sponge or beach ball to one of these people. After she has expressed her appreciation to a co-worker, she tosses the ball to someone else (anyone but the person who was just recognized), who then recognizes another staff member.

Continue this process until several people have had the opportunity to hold the recognition ball, but stop before everyone has had a chance. This avoids the situation where someone will feel left out because no one thanked him, or the need for others to come up with contrived reasons to recognize co-workers. Remind meeting participants that they can always take a moment away from the meeting to say thank you to a co-worker.

When Peer Recognition Becomes Corporate Recognition

Some companies attempt to harness the power of peer recognition with programs that invite workers to nominate colleagues for awards. While the intention is commendable, often the result is practices that have become too bureaucratic and time consuming to be useful as a way of celebrating the contributions and successes of peers.

Typically, employees submit nomination forms to a recognition committee that exists "out there somewhere" and meets periodically to adjudicate the nominations. This committee decides if what the employee did warrants recognition.

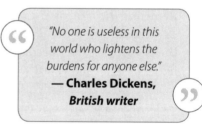

"No one is useless in this world who lightens the burdens for anyone else."
— Charles Dickens, British writer

Frequently, before the nomination reaches the committee and an award is approved, the nomination must be approved by the employee's supervisor. Without his approval, the nomination goes no further. This step serves two purposes:

- to ensure that no one is recognized if there are concerns about that person's performance
- to confirm—from the supervisor's point of view—that the person's behaviour actually deserves recognition, a requirement the reflects subtly on trust in the judgment of mere staff members.

So much time is lost during the approval process that by the time the award is presented, the recognition is no longer **Timely.** Both the nominator and the recipient have had time to forget the circumstances that prompted the recognition.

Encourage Peer Recognition, Then Get Out of the Way

A supervisor's role related to peer recognition is simple. Be the catalyst to get peer recognition going, and then step back. Let it happen. You may monitor what's going on, but don't attempt to control the recognition that occurs. Eliminate or minimize the need to judge who does and does not deserve to be recognized. Peer recognition should stand on its own. Avoid the temptation to make peer recognition part of the route to other corporate awards.

There should be few, if any rules. The easier it is, the more successful peer recognition will be. More recognition will occur. To the degree to which peer recognition needs to be administered, let the employees to run the show.

You can trust staff to know who deserves to be recognized and how best to provide that recognition.

Peer Recognition Day

Unleash the power of peer recognition within your organization by joining the movement to observe the third Tuesday of each month as Peer Recognition Day. Use this day to remind staff of the importance of recognizing their co-workers…on this day and every other day of the month.

At Least 12 Ways Supervisors Can Encourage Peer Recognition

The supervisor's role in peer recognition is to encourage, to provide opportunities and to supply the tools. Here are some things supervisors can do to facilitate peer recognition:

1. Include employees in creating a list of ways in which co-workers make their jobs easier. The resulting list will include reasons for which staff should recognize their co-workers.
2. Place thank-you cards in locations accessible to all staff. Encourage them to use these to acknowledge co-workers who help. Some may get used for personal thank-yous. Don't fret if this happens. Writing thank-you notes to anyone is good practice.

---

3. Schedule a "Positive Strokes Day" when everyone is encouraged to share positive messages with co-workers.

4. Invite staff to tell you when a co-worker has been particularly helpful. Follow up with a note to the co-worker letting her know that you are aware of what she did well.

5. Model recognition. It is infectious. When staff see you taking time regularly to praise deserving people, they will learn from this behaviour. They will begin to recognize the efforts and achievements of others more often. Encourage peer recognition by praising staff who recognize their colleagues.

6. Improve the relationship and communication among employees from different departments who depend on each other to do their work by creating awards for which employees can only nominate staff from another department who has been helpful.

7. Provide each staff member with three to five tokens of appreciation at the beginning of the week. Challenge them to give a token to every co-worker who does something that warrants recognition. When they give a token, they must tell the co-worker what she did that was deserving of recognition.

8. Provide a bulletin board or graffiti wall where peers can post messages of appreciation to their co-workers.

9. Include a few blank thank-you cards with employees' paycheques or pay advisories to remind them of the importance of recognition and encourage them to recognize their peers.

10. Provide a journal in the staff room where staff can describe how the actions of a co-worker contributed to the author's success.

11. Distribute thank-you cards at a staff meeting and encourage everyone to write at least one thank-you to a co-worker. Collect the cards and deliver them to staff members' mailboxes.

12. Designate appreciation weeks for specific groups of workers: secretaries, nurses, teachers, receptionists, cashiers, custodians, etc. Encourage co-workers to do special things for people in the group being honoured.

Worst Week Award

Sooner or later, everyone has a bad week…nothing worked out the way it should. The computer decided to demonstrate its independence. You had to deal with the customer from hell. The due dates on several projects were advanced. Not the type of memories you want to take into the weekend.

Instead of remaining stressed about the week, celebrate it with the Worst Week Award. Each week, employees compare their horror stories and decide who truly had the worst week. This person wins the Worst Week Award, which ideally should be something the winner can share with co-workers at the end of the work week: pizza, gourmet cookies, doughnuts, chocolates, a case of beer, ice cream.

By celebrating the worst of work life with co-workers instead to stewing about it all weekend, everyone looks at the work-life challenges differently. Heck, you may even look forward to the next week; maybe you can become a repeat winner of the coveted Worst Week Award.

Who Was that Masked Recognizer?

We have all heard of mystery shoppers. People are paid to pose as shoppers, while assessing the quality of services and reporting their observations, both good and bad. Why not create a team of mystery recognizers? Begin by having staff members supply some information about themselves: favourite treat, favourite flower, how they like to be recognized, favourite actor (movie or TV, alive or dead), birthday (year optional), etc. (see Chapter 6, "Not All Women Love to Shop" for more possible questions). Randomly and clandestinely provide each employee's information to a co-worker. Tell them that for the next six months (or three months or a year), they are to monitor what their assignee does, looking for opportunities to recognize that person. They can use the information you collected to personalize the recognition they provide.

But there is a catch. They are to not to reveal their identity to the person who they are responsible for recognizing. After the prescribed time expires, the identity of the mystery recognizer can be revealed, or not.

The Importance of 360-Degree Recognition

Staff recognition is frequently thought of as if it was water, that can only trickle down the managerial hierarchy. This doesn't have to be—and shouldn't be—the case. Everyone needs recognition, including supervisors, managers and executives. These are the people who are often overlooked when we talk about staff recognition. Take time to let your boss know that you appreciate her for what she does.

> *"Boss, thank you for purchasing that new computer program. It has made my job much easier and I can produce reports for clients more quickly."*

> *"Boss, thanks for adjusting my schedule so I can come in later. I really appreciate being able to be at home with my son until he leaves for school."*

> *"Boss, thank you for sitting down to talk to me about my goals. It is great to know the company is willing to help me advance my career."*

Staff recognition needs the equivalent of 360-degree appraisal systems, in which feedback is sought from people at different levels of the organization. This is often illustrated with a diagram that shows arrows representing feedback from managers, subordinates and peers converging on the individual who is the subject of the feedback.

The model for 360-degree recognition is different. Recognition radiates out in all directions from the centre. To show that recognition can flow in both directions, the individual at the centre is connected to others by two-headed arrows, showing that recognition flows both ways.

In organizations where a culture of appreciation flourishes, all staff members would have their own 360-degree recognition circles. By encouraging 360-degree recognition, organizations can ensure that all staff, no matter what their level in the organization, will be regular recipients of recognition.

"I have yet to find the man, however exalted his station, who did not do better work and put forth greater effort under a spirit of approval than under a spirit of criticism."
— Charles Schwab, *American industrialist*

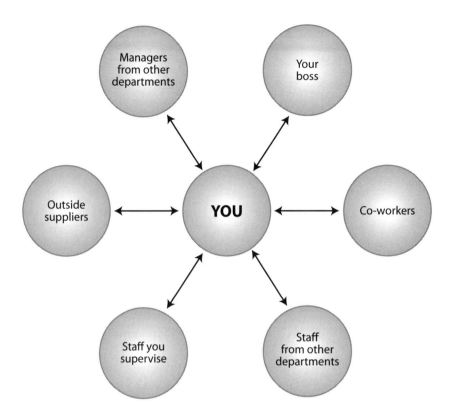

Each year, October 16 is designated as National Boss Day—also known as Bosses or Boss's Day, depending on whom you ask. This is a time to honour those men and women who supervise others. While National Boss Day is a great idea, recognition should not be a once-a-year event. We know that other staff members won't remain motivated and committed if they are only recognized once each year, so why should we expect people who just happen to be managers to be any different?

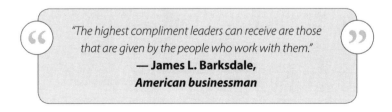

> "The highest compliment leaders can receive are those that are given by the people who work with them."
> — **James L. Barksdale,**
> **American businessman**

Chapter 14
Now That Someone has Been Hired, the Real Recruiting Begins

When children are young, we ask, "How was school?"

"It was okay, Dad."

"What did you learn?"

"Nothing."

As they grow older, our focus shifts to their work. This was the case with my son when he returned from his new job. "How was your first day?"

"Actually Dad, it's not what I expected."

This was not the response I had anticipated. He had left that morning full of excitement. This seemed to be his dream job—working in the ski and snowboard department of a local sporting goods store.

It was a job he had really wanted. While living in another city, he had spent several months working in a ski shop. He enjoyed helping customers, advising them on equipment and putting together packages. There were also the fringe benefits of learning about the latest equipment and being able to test it on the nearby mountain slopes.

"An employee is never more focused, malleable and teachable than the first day on the job."
— **Horst Schulze, *former president, Ritz-Carlton Hotels***

Returning to his hometown, he submitted an application to the sporting goods store. Receiving no response to his first application, he applied again. Still, no job offer. Finally, on his third attempt, he was interviewed and offered a job. He was delighted. He could hardly wait for his first day on the job. Unfortunately, his joy was short-lived.

When I pressed for more information, he described what had happened during his first day on the job:

- No one had explained what he was expected to do.
- He had been given simple tasks that he completed quickly, leaving him standing around, unsure of what to do next. Rather than suggesting what needed to be done, managers appeared disgusted that he was idle.
- He was told specifically that he was to operate within strict guidelines from which he was unable to deviate without permission from a manager. That left him unable to empower himself to act in the best interest of the customer as he had done so often in his previous job.
- He received no feedback, either positive or negative, on what he did.

"The job is okay for now," he concluded. "Until I find something else." It was his first day, but already he was preparing to search for a new job.

This is not how managers and supervisors want new employees to feel. They want them to leave at the end of that first day feeling an enhanced sense of excitement about their work, where they work, and the people with whom they work. New staff should feel committed to the organization, believing they are already making a contribution and will continue to add to the organization's success. When their family or friends ask about their first day, they should respond positively:

> *"It is a great place to work. I really like the people I work with. They seem to care about each other and they already care about me. They asked me to do things that were important. It was only my first day, but I feel that I am contributing. I am looking forward to going to work tomorrow."*

What went wrong in this example? How was the excitement of the new job replaced with disillusionment in one short day? As a supervisor, what can you do to ensure this is not how new staff members think about your organization following their first day on the job?

Day One: The Most Important Day of an Employee's Career

The sporting goods store owner failed to understand the importance of what happens during an employee's first day. Like many others, he felt that once someone is hired, the recruitment process is over. In fact, the task of re-recruiting staff has just begun. Re-recruiting is necessary to retain staff, to keep them motivated and engaged, and to minimize turnover. It should begin on Day One.

For most new staff members, just starting a new job is motivating. They want to be successful—to do their jobs well. They want to feel that they are contributing, right away. From Day One, they want to confirm the wisdom of the person who hired them. They want to be noticed for what they are doing and how well they are doing it.

Make Day One a rewarding experience so that by the end of the shift the newcomer will be looking forward to the next morning. When supervisors fail to make a newcomer's first day special, the motivation associated with the new job begins to fade.

"For many of us, the most hopeful day on the job is our first."
— **Gary Heil, Tom Parker and Deborah C. Stephens,** ***One Size Fits One***

The desire to do well is replaced with a resolve to comply to minimum requirements. The newcomer does only enough to get by and to avoid negative feedback.

On Day One, and on the days leading up to and following Day One, organizations plant the seeds of employee retention or resignation. The manager's job in dealing with a new employee is similar to the relationship between an effective salesperson and his customers. The sale (hiring) doesn't end when the customer pays and accepts delivery. Effective salespeople follow up with after-sales service, to ensure that the customer is happy with her purchase and is taking advantage of all that the new product can do. He reinforces the customer's buying decision. There is no opportunity to become disillusioned with the purchase (or the decision to accept the job offer).

The process of re-recruitment works in the same fashion. The focus of the recruiting process shifts from attracting applicants to retaining those who are hired. Supervisors re-recruit by reinforcing the newcomer's decision to accept the job offer. They let newcomers know that what they do is important, and that they and their contributions are valued. Retaining quality hires is a process of continuous recruiting of applicants who are now employees.

Few employees come to a new company planning to stay for life. Among many of the people with whom I once worked, it was common to hear, "When I came, I only planned to stay two years for the experience. Then I intended to move on to something else." Some did leave within two years, but others stayed on long after those first two years were over.

Knowing the value of positive first impressions, it is important that the process of welcoming new staff be taken seriously and be well-planned. At no time is an employee more at risk of leaving than during the first few weeks and months, before a bond is established between the employee and his employer. Turnover rates are typically highest among new staff.

A good orientation program—or "onboarding" if you prefer the more trendy term—can improve retention rates. Everything that the newcomer experiences during the orientation process should confirm the wisdom of his decision to accept your job offer. Your organization is where he was meant to be. There are compelling reasons for him to remain.

The orientation period is a time to build comfort and rapport. It is also a time to acquaint the newcomer with the organization and its culture. There is no better place to begin than by explaining and promoting the beliefs and values that drive the organization.

"People come and go so quickly here."
**— Dorothy,
The Wizard of Oz**

Orientation activities serve to educate and inspire new employees. It is a time to define expectations, ensuring that employees begin their new jobs with a clear understanding of their roles within the organization. Understanding what is expected of them prepares employees to act in ways that contribute to both their own successes and that of the organization.

Effective orientations for new employees are not a one-day event, but a process that continues over days and weeks. Some aspects of the orientation may begin before the employee's first day on the job, while others may not be completed until well into the first year on the job. The process of welcoming new staff can begin as soon as the person accepts the formal employment offer. Let the newly-hired employees know that the organization is looking forward to their arrival.

While human resources professionals may take the lead in planning and conducting orientations, the welcoming of new staff is too important to be left to just one group. Others, from senior executives to front-line co-workers have a role to play. Whether or not they are formally involved, all will contribute to creating the newcomer's first impressions.

The role played by the supervisor is most important. She is key to the effectiveness of the newcomer's welcome. The new employee will relate to his supervisor on a day-to-day basis. How the supervisor treats employees on their first day can have a powerful and lasting effect, setting the tone for what may be a long-term work relationship. When employees are made to feel ignored, unappreciated or a bother on their first day, they will begin to think about finding their next job, rather than committing to their current one. They want to be where they are valued as individuals, not just seen as another cog in the corporate machine.

Supervisors who schedule time with new employees on their first day and during their first weeks convey a message of respect. Showing respect for the newcomer is important. People leave places where they do not feel respected. Time that supervisors spend with newcomers is time well spent.

Key Day One Messages

The key purpose of the orientation is to educate new hires about the expectations of the job, the purpose and values of the organization, and how and where the new staff member fits. Doing so lays the foundation for making recognition **Relevant.** Here are some messages that new employees should hear on Day One, or certainly within the first week:

- **Here are our expectations of you:** Review the job description. Clarify anything that is vague. Talk about behaviours that are **Relevant** to doing the job well. Explain that staff recognition focuses on actions that contribute to on-the-job success.
- **Recognition is part of our culture:** Employees should expect to be recognized frequently by their supervisor and co-workers. In turn, they will be expected to thank those with whom they work when it is deserved. Suggest reasons they may wish to acknowledge others and ways to express this recognition. Make them aware of the organization's recognition programs and the criteria for awards.
- **Feedback will be Timely:** Let new employees know that you will be monitoring their work because you want to let people know when they have done well...or not so well. Whether positive or negative, they will receive feedback frequently and as soon after the behaviour is observed as possible. You won't save up to dump a pile of out-of-context feedback on them every few months.

Answer This Question Before it is Asked

Most of us who make hiring decisions have been asked at one time or another by an unsuccessful candidate, "Why didn't I get the job?" A much less common question is the one asked by the person who had just been hired: "Why did I get the job?"

Don't wait to be asked this second question! New employees may be uncertain why they were hired. On Day One, or even sooner, meet with the new employee. Explain why she was hired. What did you like in her resume or in what you heard during her interview? What special skills, knowledge or attitudes did you identify during the selection process that caused you to choose her over other applicants? What skills do you feel she can bring to her new position?

> " *We discovered the key to patient satisfaction is to focus not on patients first, but on your employees. We quickly realized that the satisfaction of our patients was directly related to the satisfaction of our employees; only happy, fulfilled employees will provide the highest level of health care to our patients.* "
> — **Al Stubblefield,**
> ***The Baptist Health Care Journey to Excellence*** "

This dose of positives will get the newcomer off to a good start. You have to let her know that she is valued for the knowledge and skills she can contribute to the organization. Show your ongoing commitment to her development by discussing her career goals and how your organization may be able to help her reach these goals.

The process of recognizing staff and letting them know they are valued should begin on Day One and continue as long as they work there. Because we always identify positives about candidates before we hire them, feedback based on the interview is a great way to begin.

Some Tasks Should Never be Delegated

Today, more than a quarter-century later, I still remember meeting with my supervisor on my first day in a new job. After explaining what was expected of me, he made an offer that demonstrated his commitment to my success:

> *"If you have any questions about the job, please come and see me. I have told my secretary that if you want to see me any time during the next few weeks, she is to find a way to work you into my schedule."*

As I was getting to know my new job, there were several times when I took him up on his offer. And true to his word, there was always time in his day for us to meet.

"Start with good people, lay out the rules, communicate with your employees, motivate them and reward them. If you do all those things effectively, you can't miss."
— Lee Iacocca, American businessman and author

This story illustrates how important the supervisor is in making a new employee feel like a valued member of the organization. As a supervisor, you are key to the integration of new employees. There are two tasks related to welcoming new staff that should not be assigned to others: making the job offer and greeting the new employee.

The most important call a future employee will receive is that in which he receives a job offer. The offer should come from someone the new staff member will see as significant and having authority and importance in the organization, such as you, his soon-to-be direct supervisor. The newcomer should feel that he is important enough to warrant a call from the boss.

The supervisor should also be available on the employee's first day. By scheduling time to greet the new employee, introduce him to others and talk about the company, the supervisor sends a message to both the new person and to existing staff: the newcomer is valued enough that the supervisor has set aside time to be with him. This adds to the newcomer's credibility in the eyes of co-workers.

As important as it is that you are there to greet the new employee at the beginning of the day, it is equally important that you spend time with her near the end of Day One. Discuss the day. Ask questions:

- How are things going? Is anything worrying you?
- Have you felt welcomed here? What have we done to make you feel welcome?
- What have you learned about our organization or your work?
- How were you able to contribute?
- What questions do you have about our company?

This is also a good time for you to provide specific, positive feedback on something you saw the newcomer do well. A new employee should hear words of acknowledgement as soon as possible—preferably before Day One

145

ends, and certainly during the first week. Find a reason to recognize a new-comer for a contribution or achievement. This message will be appreciated during those first few hours and days of uncertainty and stress.

Don't wait for the new employee to make a major contribution before rec-ognizing her for the first time. Find some small thing she has done well and recognize her for that. If the novice has been successful in learning her job, recognize her for this success.

Day One would be a good time to introduce the concept of peer recogni-tion. When you meet with her near the end of the day, ask whether any co-worker has been particularly helpful. What did he do? Give the newcomer a blank thank-you card and encourage her to take a moment to write a brief note of appreciation to this co-worker.

The Day One discussion should be the first of a series of conversations that you will have with the newcomer over the first several weeks, as she settles into her job. Schedule time weekly to reflect on the past week and preview the next. These meetings are also times to assess the newcomer's progress and provide feedback. Everything should be discussed as it occurs. There should be no surprises during the performance appraisal at the end of her probationary period.

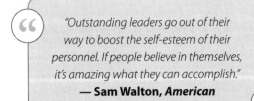

"Outstanding leaders go out of their way to boost the self-esteem of their personnel. If people believe in themselves, it's amazing what they can accomplish."
— Sam Walton, *American businessman*

At Least 9 Ways to Welcome Staff on Day One

Here are some things that you, as the newcomer's supervisor, can do on Day One to help the newcomer feel welcome:

1. Before the newcomer's first day, ask her some of the questions that can be used to make recognition **Appropriate** (See Chapter 6, "Not All Women Love to Shop"). Have her favourite treat waiting, along with a note of welcome.

2. Display a sign in the reception area (where it will be the first thing the newcomer sees) that welcomes her by name.

3. Give the newcomer a tour. Point out key locations: the lunchroom, washrooms, parking locations, the photocopier area, your office. Tell him about fire exits and muster points in case the building needs to be evacuated. The safety of new employees is important.

4. Introduce the newcomer to other staff, especially those she will be working with most closely. Tell them that this person has much to offer and will be a real asset to the team. Use phrases such as, "We are pleased that Sue decided to join our staff," or, "Jim brings some new ideas that I think may help us serve customers even better."

5. Tell the newcomer one interesting, non-work-related "fact" about each employee to whom he is introduced. This may help him remember his new co-workers and may become the topic of future informal conversations.

6. Present the newcomer with a company lapel pin. Make the presentation special. Highlight the significance of the pin. "This pin represents all that we at Big School District stand for, our goals and our values. Wear it with pride."

7. Provide the newcomer with the supplies and equipment he needs to get down to work. He should not spend his first days on the job searching for the tools he needs. Let him know where to find more supplies when required.

8. Introduce the newcomer to customers he will be serving. Before meeting the customer, be sure to bring the newcomer up-to-speed on anything she needs to know about the customer to serve him well.

   "Ms. James will be looking after your account. She has a great deal of experience and a good understanding of our industry. I have reviewed your ordering history with her. I am confident that she can deal effectively with all your requests."

9. Set a goal for the newcomer that she should be able to accomplish within a few days. This allows her to feel in control of her work. Completing the task successfully will give the newcomer a sense of accomplishment (and you a reason to recognize her).

Chapter 15
Punished for Success

The executive was quite frank about a top performer's chances for advancement. It wasn't going to happen!

The executive's words may be surprising, but the underlying feelings are understandable. Typically, top performers are the ones who are promoted. In health care, top nurses move into administrative positions. Great teachers land up in the principal's office. Productive sales people become sales managers. Each leaves a huge gap in the wake of her promotion.

Douglas was one of those top performers. After several years in a front-line position, he felt it was time to move up the corporate ladder. No one could argue that Douglas didn't have the right stuff to become a supervisor. He had enough experience, knew the company inside out, had the respect of his colleagues and the loyalty of customers. He had taken college courses at his own expense to develop his leadership potential.

He had everything the organization said was important for new managers to possess. But he wasn't going to be promoted any time soon. Douglas was too valuable in his current position to be promoted.

"We could never promote him," said the executive. "He does such a good job. Our customers would never forgive us."

The recognition that Douglas received for doing a good job was to be denied the opportunity for advancement. There was to be no increase in pay or status within the organization for him. Douglas was being punished for his success.

Other employees in other organizations have received similar "rewards" for doing what is expected of them:

- People who arrive for the scheduled start time are destined to wait for latecomers before meetings are called to order.
- The manager of a successful, smoothly operating store is transferred to another store that is plagued by low sales, high staff turnover and a serious problem with shoplifters.
- Each fall, the teacher who has a record of success with difficult students is assigned other students with reputations for being disruptive underachievers.
- Top-producing salespeople are reassigned to a territory where sales have been low for years.
- Frugal managers who produce budget surpluses one year are given less money to work with for the next.

When the Going Gets Tough...

"Whenever we have a really tough job, you are my go-to guy," the boss explains before assigning yet another thorny problem that is going to require extra time and effort to resolve. For a while, knowing that the boss is confident in one's ability to handle the really difficult jobs is good for one's self-esteem. But the lustre soon begins to fade.

Eventually, top performers tire of receiving only the most challenging assignments, while all around, others are given easier tasks. They watch co-workers leave at the end of the day while they remain behind to work on their special projects.

Just this once, couldn't the top performer be given a simple task? Isn't it about time that her colleagues were asked to devote extra time and effort to completing one of those projects that seem to be reserved for top performers?

While no organization would intentionally do anything that would cause its top performers to leave, the practice of always assigning tough tasks to them may actually be having that effect. A recent study by Leadership IQ found that the very people who make organizations successful are the ones most likely to be actively searching for a new job.

"Accomplishing the impossible means only that the boss will add it to your regular duties."
— **Doug Larson,**
American columnist

A Promotion Can Be a Punishment

Some staff members welcome promotions as acknowledgement of success in their current positions. For others, unwanted or untimely promotions can be as much of a punishment as denying promotions to those who have earned the right to advancement. They don't want to be promoted, simply because they enjoy their work and want to continue doing what they do.

In some cases, the timing may be bad. The staff member may have increased family responsibilities, such as young children or an ailing parent. He may have health problems of his own. Maybe the staff member has just committed to returning to school part time and wishes to avoid any additional work responsibilities until these studies have been completed.

Whatever the reason, a promotion may not be the best way to recognize a productive staff member. Be sensitive to the staff member's circumstances. Allow the person to say "No" without risk of penalty. Avoid pressuring a top performer to say "Yes."

"If you turn down this promotion, you may never be offered another." Don't say it! Don't even think it!

In response to a survey, nearly half (47 per cent) of employees who were classified as top performers, based on annual performance appraisals, admitted they were submitting resumes and going for interviews. Even more disturbing is the finding that they are being driven to leave by their managers.

"The worst part of this is that we typically cause our high performers to quit by how we treat them," says Mark Murphy, Leadership IQ's CEO.

"Frankly, we treat our high performers worse than any other employee," he says. "When a manager has a tough project upon which the whole company depends, to whom do they turn? Who gets the late hours and the stress? It's not the low performers, because managers want the project done right. Instead, managers turn to their handful of high performers. Over and over we ask them to go above and beyond, making their jobs tough and burning them out at a terrible pace. Meanwhile, low performers often get easier jobs because their bosses dread dealing with them and may avoid them altogether."

And how likely is it that these low performers, who the organization might even benefit from losing, are looking for a new position?

Not very, according to the study. Only 18 per cent of low performers and 25 per cent of middle performers were actually looking for other work.

Without the opportunity for promotion, Douglas found the change he wanted in another way. He accepted a lateral transfer within the company to a position where he was still in contact with his customers. There, he bided his time. When a supervisory position was advertised by a rival organization, he applied.

Douglas was interviewed and hired. Shortly after he joined this new company, his manager was promoted and Douglas succeeded him as department head.

What about those customers that so concerned the executive where Douglas worked previously? The ones that would never forgive them if Douglas had been promoted? How forgiving are they now that Douglas works elsewhere? For that matter, are they still customers or did they follow Douglas to the rival company?

Who is being punished now?

"What's the use you learning to do right, when it's troublesome to do right and ain't no trouble to do wrong, and the wages is just the same?"
— Mark Twain, *The Adventures of Huckleberry Finn*

At Least 6 Ways to Avoid Punishing
Top Performers for Their Success

1. Make top performers aware of future projects and invite them to choose their next assignments.
2. Don't block promotions that involve transfers to another department because you don't want to loose a top performer. Your department's loss may be another department's gain, but the whole organization will continue to benefit from the top performer's efforts and you may be perceived within the organization as a developer of top talent.
3. Monitor staff members' workloads. If you notice that what someone is doing is affecting her work/life balance negatively, discuss it with her.
4. Restrain yourself from always assigning the most difficult tasks to the same few top performers, just because you know they will do it right.
5. When a promotion is not an option, find ways to enrich the staff member's job without increasing his workload. Provide variety. Offer more autonomy or control over the work. Allow the staff member to make more work-related decisions. Give the staff member responsibility for managing a small budget. Make training opportunities available. Focus on ways for the staff member to grow professionally.
6. Don't promote people who don't want to be promoted.

"By working faithfully eight hours a day you may eventually get to be boss and work twelve hours a day."
— **Robert Frost,** *American poet*

Chapter 16
What I Learned From Dan's Mother

I learned an important lesson about staff recognition from a woman I never met. I did meet her son, but only once.

Dan, a 50-something gas company employee, came to our home a few years ago to inspect our furnace. Impressed by Dan's customer service, I featured him as a "Service Star" in *Briefly Noted,* the newsletter I distribute to clients and other subscribers.

> ### Read Dan's story at:
> www.seaconsultingonline.com/Articles/Service/star_13.htm).

Having written the column, I might never have thought much about Dan again had his manager not been a subscriber. The boss let me know that he had shared the newsletter with Dan, who had then sent a copy to his mother.

A few weeks later, there was a voice mail waiting for me when I returned to my office. Hesitantly, with nervousness evident in her voice, a woman began by referring to the article about Dan, summarizing its key points. As the message played out, she seemed to gain confidence. She thanked me for what I had written. She concluded by proudly proclaiming, "I am Dan's mother."

What an epiphany! Parents want to be proud of their children, whether they are preschoolers or adults well-established in their careers. Parents want to know their children are doing well in whatever they do.

Parents often rely on others to provide them with reasons to be proud. They need teachers to tell them when their children are doing well in their studies. They need coaches to describe their success in hockey, soccer or baseball. They need Scout and Girl Guide leaders to recall how well they did during their first camping experience.

From the time their offspring get their first after-school or weekend job, parents want to know their children are performing well in the workplace. Knowing their children perform well in a fast-food restaurant or for a retailer reflects well on their upbringing. Parents can feel proud of how their kids turned out.

In February 2007, I told the story of Dan's mother when speaking at a teachers' convention in Calgary. After the presentation, a teacher approached me. She had a story to tell.

During one of her mother's visits from out-of-town, the teacher had taken her mother on a tour of her school. As they were moving through the school, they encountered the principal. Introductions completed, the principal turned to the young teacher's mother. He wanted her to know how much he appreciated having her daughter on staff. He described her contributions to student learning.

The mother never forgot those words of praise. Whenever the teacher was feeling down about teaching and questioning whether she should continue in her profession, her mother would remind her of what the principal had said. It must have worked. The daughter was still teaching.

Supervisors may never meet the parents of their staff, but this doesn't mean they can't let parents know their child is doing well. As a supervisor, you could do this through a phone call or in a letter to the parents. Describe what their child is doing well. Let them know she is a valued member of the staff and appreciated for what she does. Give them credit for doing such a good job raising their child. They should be proud of how she turned out.

"Moms like polite kids. Try to have nice manners. Use 'please' and 'thank you' and 'may I.' Ask to be excused from the table and wipe your face."
— **Alec Greven, *9-year-old author of How to Talk to Moms***

Parents can become unexpected allies in a supervisor's efforts to retain staff. When their family member is frustrated about the job, they can remind them that they are valued where they are now. "Stay where you are appreciated, rather than going somewhere else."

Dan's mother's voice-mail message also demonstrated that the need to feel proud of a child's success isn't limited to parents of younger workers. All parents want to know that their children are successful in their chosen careers.

Become the messenger of this good news. While Mother's Day and Father's Day are obvious times to give parents of your staff members reasons to be proud, you shouldn't limit yourself to these once-a-year occasions. Letting parents know about their children's contributions can occur any time during the year.

Calendar Opportunities for Family-Focused Recognition

Family Day – a holiday in some Canadian provinces
(third Monday in February)

Mother's Day (second Sunday in May)

Father's Day (third Sunday in June)

Grandparent's Day (First Sunday after Labour Day)

So far, I have only written about the parents of staff members, but families consist of more than just parents. Other family members, such as a spouse, children and grandparents, may be even more important in your staff members' lives. Include these other family members in your family-focused recognition plans. Family-focused recognition demonstrates your understanding of the importance of family to staff members.

Whether the cause is the aftermath to the attacks of 9/11, or a different generation with different values coming to dominate the workplace, there seems to be a shift in how employees view work/life balance. While work remains important, other aspects of life are seen as increasingly important. This includes a greater emphasis on family.

Shift work and requirements to work evenings or weekends are common in the modern workplace. Some positions involve work-related travel. Many people carry briefcases home at the end of the day. Nurses may be called in for overtime shifts. Police officers or gas company employees may be summoned to deal with emergencies in the middle of night. Teachers spend evenings and weekends marking assignments and planning lessons. At times, employees must cancel vacations at the last minute. Cell phones and email tie employees to the job 24/7. All of this means that workers might miss family events, school concerts or their kids' sports activities.

The adage that, "Behind every successful man there is a woman," is likely no longer politically correct. Nevertheless, the underlying sentiment remains as true today as it ever has been. Staff members who have the support of family members—parents, wives and husbands, children—will be more productive on the job. With family support, it is easier for employees to deal with work-related disruptions to family life.

Managers and supervisors can contribute to creating family understanding and support by seeing those with whom they work as employees second, but people first— individuals with lives away from work that often include families.

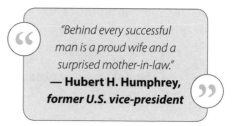

"Behind every successful man is a proud wife and a surprised mother-in-law."
— **Hubert H. Humphrey,**
former U.S. vice-president

Building family support and understanding for the demands of work begins with managers acknowledging and demonstrating that they comprehend the importance of families.

One of the common themes among organizations that are identified by publications and associations as the best places to work is that they are family-friendly. Family-friendly workplaces are characterized as offering flexible work arrangements (tele-work, flextime, job sharing, compressed work weeks and part-time work), employee and family assistance programs, child and eldercare services, health and welfare initiatives, and leaves-of-absence to deal with family-related matters.

Changing the Nature of Schoolyard Conversations

While much of what is done to build family understanding and support is focused on adults, one should not forget the importance of building support among children. They long for parents who are absent due to work demands, to return and spend more time with them. And just as parents, such as Dan's mother, need reasons to be proud of their children, children want to be proud of their parents.

Think of those, "my-dad-can-beat-up-your-dad" arguments in the schoolyard. They are rooted in the need to have pride in parents—who they are, what they do and what they have accomplished. Supervisors and managers can provide reasons to be proud by writing notes to children of their employees, thanking them for sharing their mothers or fathers and describing how they contribute to the company. Such correspondence could change the tone of playground conversations.

"My dad works harder at his job than your dad does."

"No, he doesn't."

"Does too."

"Does not."

"Does. His boss said so."

"She didn't."

"She did. She wrote me a letter. She thanked me for sharing my dad. She said he works really hard and how happy she is that he works for her department."

"Wow! You're lucky! My dad's boss never writes me any letters. I guess you're right. Your dad does work harder than my dad."

In 2001, I witnessed a professional association make a family part of the celebration of a member's contributions to the profession.

At its annual convention that year, the National Speakers' Association presented its highest award—the Cavett—to Zig Ziglar. While the award was a surprise to Ziglar, it wasn't to several family members who were invited to the awards ceremony and were hidden backstage as the award was announced. As the renowned speaker began his acceptance speech, family members quietly moved onto the stage, standing where he couldn't see them, but within clear view of audience. The audience began to applaud even before the speaker concluded his remarks.

Obviously puzzled by this reaction, Ziglar turned to see what was happening behind him. A grin spread across his face. It was clear that he appreciated having his family there to share in this important event.

The NSA provides a model others could emulate. Involve family members when recognizing staff. Invite them to attend recognition ceremonies. Thank them for the support that enabled the recipient to be successful. Doing so demonstrates to family members that the importance of their support is recognized and appreciated. It also shows the employee being honoured, and others who witness or hear about the event, that the organization understands the importance of family.

At Least 17 Ways to Provide Family-Focused Recognition

1. Send employees' parents notes on Mother's or Father's Day describing what staff members do well and thanking them for doing such a good job of raising their child—your employee.

2. Send flowers to a new staff member's home on his first day.

3. Send flowers or another small gift to a staff member's partner when your employee has had to work extra hours on a big project.

4. Offer an employee who has been travelling on company business an evening out with his or her spouse, in the form of theatre or movie tickets, or a gift certificate for dinner at a favourite restaurant.

5. Send a thank-you gift to the staff member's family, such as a fruit basket for the family, a toy or book for a child, flowers or a bottle of wine for a spouse. Add a note that says, "Thank you for sharing your parent/spouse/child."

6. Be generous about allowing staff members extended periods of paid or unpaid leave to deal with family matters.

7. Find out the ages of staff members' children and send them cards or small gifts on their birthdays.

8. Send a gift to parents (or grandparents) of a new baby, perhaps the baby's first book, inscribed with a message describing how much the parent or grandparent is valued by your organization.

9. Provide staff members with coupons for time off to attend a concert or to volunteer at their children's (or grandchildren's) school.

10. Send greeting cards to family members on appropriate occasions, such as birthdays and anniversaries.

11. Send sympathy or get well cards to family members when appropriate.

12. Send congratulations cards for births, when children graduate or when they get their first jobs.

13. Take a photo of a staff member at his workplace and mail it to his family. "Just our way of letting you know that we appreciate what your father/son/husband does at work."

14. Leave a message of appreciation on a staff member's voice mail at home, where a family member may be the first to hear it.

15. Arrange for a family portrait that can be displayed on the staff member's desk.

16. Celebrate milestones in the lives of staff members: weddings, births, anniversaries, birthdays, retirements, and graduations

17. Grieve and provide support during difficult times: illnesses, the deaths of a family member, loss of a pet

Chapter 17
Everything Before the "But" is...

A Message for Nelson's 97-year-old Mother

Hi Mom,

Have you enjoyed the book so far? I hope you feel proud of me for writing it, just like Dan's mother, who I wrote about in the last chapter, felt proud of her son. Because I don't want to change how you feel, I would like you to skip this chapter. Please, just go on to the next chapter. It's a good one! One of my favourites.

When we were kids, you warned us not to use certain words—bad words, swear words. And I usually don't, but one just slipped in when I was writing this chapter. Actually, someone else said it, but I still don't want you to see it. You might be upset with me for using it. After all, I didn't have to quote him.

So, don't read this chapter. **_Please!!_**

With love,

Nelson (your son)

At halftime, a TV sportscaster approached the coach of a football team. The team had had several early-season wins and was well on its way to another victory. The brief interview went something like this:

Interviewer: You must be pleased with your team's performance so far in today's game. They scored five touchdowns in the first half.

Coach: Yeah, five touchdowns are good, but we missed a field goal. That is not acceptable. We should do better.

Imagine if this coach was your boss. What message would you take from his comments? Likely not that he was happy with what you had achieved. What you would have heard is that you had not done well enough. Your level of performance was unacceptable.

Managers and supervisors make similar comments in workplaces everyday:

"You did a nice job on that report, *but* it should have been completed sooner."

"These are great results, *but* it would have been easier if you had done it the way I said."

"The sales figures for the first quarter are up, *but* they are still less than what we had hoped for."

"The operation was a success, *but* the patient died."

But Aren't We Here to Honour Our Staff?

Sometimes there is a disconnect between what is said from the podium, and seating arrangements at service awards events.

Speakers at these events follow a predictable script. "You are our most important asset. This evening is all about you."

Except when it came to assigning seats for the banquet. Often the best tables, those that will be served first, are reserved for the organization's VIPs—executives, members of the board of directors, etc. By setting aside a special area, you may unintentionally create an us-versus-them atmosphere.

On the other hand, by encouraging board members and executives to sit among the real VIPs—staff who are being honoured—you convey a message that staff members are genuinely valued for their contributions, achievements and service.

In these examples, the supervisors may have acknowledged success, but then they quickly shifted the focus to what wasn't achieved. For them, the glass is half empty. In the case of the coach, he saw the glass as one-eighth empty when only a full glass would do.

When praise is followed immediately by criticism it creates the impression that what was done was not done well enough. Linking praise to a negative comment diminishes the value of praise for a job well done. The praise does not seem **Genuine.**

Hearing the word "but" puts staff on the defensive. When we hear the word "but," the immediate response is to believe that the words that follow will be the most important. We remember best what we last heard.

Repeated messages that follow praise with criticism can be demoralizing, create self-doubt and lower productivity.

"I didn't do enough."

"I should have done better."

"I am not good enough at my job."

Meanwhile, back on the field for the second half, the football team went on to a lopsided victory over its opponent.

By the next game a week later, the coach's halftime comments must have reached the players. They seemed less fired up as they took to the field and played with less enthusiasm. The result was a loss, which proved to be only the first in a losing streak that continued until the end of the season. When the season ended, there was one more loss to come—the coach lost his job. He was fired because the team had ceased to be productive.

And fittingly so. While public criticism is part of a professional athlete's life, it can still be embarrassing. Embarrassment is a strong emotion that is not soon forgotten. It is hard to trust someone who has embarrassed us. This is not someone who an employee will approach for advice or coaching. A manager or supervisor who staff perceives as untrustworthy is not someone who can successfully motivate them to work hard, become more productive, or win football games.

Praise should stand on its own. After recognizing a staff member for her contributions or achievements, stop talking. Allow her time to absorb the good feelings that recognition releases. Let her enjoy the moment. This is not the time to point out shortcomings in her performance.

There are, of course, times when negative feedback and reprimands are appropriate. In these cases, the negative message should also stand on its on, without including a few empty words of praise intended to soften the blow of the negative message. Staff will see this for what it is— just blowing smoke. Such praise is seen as insincere and will hamper the supervisor's ability to provide **Genuine** recognition in the future.

 "My philosophy is to never start talking about 'if' or 'but' or the past, because 90 per cent of what follows will be negative."
— **Gordie Howe, *legendary hockey superstar***

During her lifetime, Mary Kay Ash was saluted for her business success and wisdom in dealing with people. But amongst all the good advice she offered, there was one suggestion on providing feedback that I feel was simply wrong: "Sandwich every criticism between two layers of praise." Staff will soon catch on to what's happening and will quickly become skeptical about praise and recognition, because they anticipate that every time they hear positive words, these will be followed by negatives—the message that the supervisor really wants to get across. Every time staff hears words of praise spoken by this supervisor, they prepare for the other shoe to fall. Praise and recognition should not be used to buffer criticism.

There are some occasions when both positive and negative feedback can occur at the same time. The most obvious is during performance appraisals. In this context, staff members arrive for the meeting anticipating that they will hear their supervisor describe successes and suggest areas for improvement.

 "The meanest, most contemptible kind of praise is that which first speaks well of a man, and then qualifies it with a 'but.'"
— **Henry Ward Beecher, *American clergyman and social reformer***

Another place where praise may be used effectively is following a reprimand. Having reached agreement that improvement is required, the supervisor could express confidence in the employee's ability to change, based on how well she has done previously. "I recall how you tackled the issue related to your record keeping in the spring. Based on what I saw then, I know you are up for this challenge. I am confident in your ability to make the change we discussed."

While but is a powerful tool that supervisors use to yank back praise and recognition, there are other ways in which supervisors diminish the value of recognition.

A few weeks into her new job, Christina received a message from another department, praising her for the way she had done her job. Excitedly, she approached the woman who had been assigned to mentor her.

The mentor's response was not what Christina had anticipated. Rather than using this as an opportunity to reinforce the positive feedback, the mentor saw Christina's good news as evidence of the success of her coaching. "I guess that shows what a good job I did of training you."

Then, there are those supervisors who shift the focus to their past successes. After a brief reference to the person whose performance they are suppose to be acknowledging, the supervisor begins to reminisce about his own experiences. "A few years ago, I had a similar experience. I recall how well I responded to solve the problem…" Soon he is lost in his memories and oblivious to the person whose recent actions he was supposed to praise.

The value of recognition and praise is lost when it is followed by:

- A request to undertake a new task
- An inquiry about progress on another project
- A change of focus to an unrelated topic

When these focus shifts become normal practice, recognition recipients can't hear the positive words because they are already preparing themselves for the requests that are coming. When this happens, the recognition appears insincere. It is not **Genuine**. Recognition is seen as being used to "soften up" the recipient to make him want or feel he must undertake another task.

The only time it would be acceptable to move to another topic is when the recipient leads the conversation in that direction.

The word "but," whether spoken or implied, has no place near any expression of appreciation. As a former colleague once told me. "Everything before the 'but' is…

Bullshit!"

Sorry Mom!

> Road apples!
> Mule muffins!
> Mule fritters!
> Monkey muffins!
> Buffalo bagels!
> Buffalo chips!
> Pigeon pellets!
> Pony pucks!
> Beaver biscuits!
> Cow cookies!
> Bull cookies!
> Pig feathers!
> **— Colonel Sherman T. Potter, M*A*S*H 4077**

DIY RECOGNITION RESEARCH:
The Sandwich Question

What you will need for this research project:
A few friends, family members or work colleagues (also works with complete strangers)

Research Process:
1. Ask, "Describe the last sandwich you had."
2. Listen to the responses. How did they begin their description? Did they think about the filling—turkey, egg salad, veggies, or ham and cheese? Or did they begin by describing the bread?

Implications for the Workplace:
When it comes to ordering a sandwich, most of us begin with a request for a specific filling. The choice of bread that will hold it together is usually an afterthought. The same is true when we "sandwich criticism between two layers of praise." What do the recipients remember? For that matter, what do you want them to remember best?

Hint: Avoid sending confusing messages. Praise when it's warranted; reprimand when it's required. Don't mix the two.

Chapter 18
Everyone Knows About the Principal's Office

I froze when I heard a male voice on the grocery store's intercom.

"Joanne...come to the office."

Just those five words transported me back several decades to junior high school. I experienced the same feelings I recall experiencing as a student — first relief, then fear. Relief that it hadn't been my name that everyone heard, but fear that I would be called next.

How many of my fellow shoppers had thoughts similar to my own?

"This can't be good. What did Joanne do? Something bad is going to happen to her."

Being called to the manager's office is like being called to the principal's office. Even if their names had never been called, most students anticipated that their turn would come.

Being called to the office is among those moments we dread, along with times when:

- a police officer appears at the door unexpectedly
- we receive a late-night telephone call from a relative
- a doctor who promised to call, "if there are any problems," before sending you for medical tests, does

There were, of course, several reasons why the manager might have wanted to see Joanne in his office that had nothing to do with her having done something wrong. Perhaps he wanted:

- To ask her opinion before making an important decision
- To praise her for helping an elderly customer complete her shopping
- To seek her input before setting next month's work schedule
- To congratulate her on a promotion

Staff believe that anyone who is called to the manager's office is in trouble, just as students expect that classmates are "in for it" if they were called to the principal's office—or worse yet, to the office of the vice principal in charge of discipline. People are called to the privacy of an office when they are to be reprimanded or told that they are being laid off. This is how it should be. It is inappropriate for a manager to reprimand an employee in front of co-workers or customers, even though many of us have witnessed such behaviour. This is managerial misconduct, which is destructive to an employee's dignity and self-esteem. Public reprimands are more likely to build resentment than commitment to change and improvement.

Experience has taught us that if the manager had had good news to deliver to Joanne, he might have left the office to seek her out and recognize her in public, in front of her colleagues. Doing so can

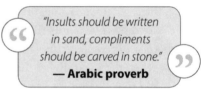

"Insults should be written in sand, compliments should be carved in stone."
— **Arabic proverb**

enhance an employee's dignity and self-esteem and increase her commitment to doing the job well. When it is **Relevant** to the organization's purpose and on-the-job success, and includes an **Explicit** description of what the employee did, public recognition serves as a reminder of expectations—both to those who witness the recognition and to the recipient.

Likely, when she heard her name, Joanne understood the distinction between what commonly happens in public and what happens in private. Her colleagues understand this. Shoppers understand this. In light of this nearly universal understanding, the logical conclusion was that Joanne had been summoned to the office because she had done something wrong. She was in trouble.

While reprimands and other bad news should always be delivered in private, there is no reason that recognition should occur only in public. Good news can be delivered in the privacy of the manager's office. In fact, I believe this should occur regularly.

Recognition delivered in private may appear—and actually may be—more **Genuine** than recognition that is delivered in public. The manager is not "playing to the audience" of the recipient's co-workers. The only focus of private recognition is the person whose contributions are being acknowledged.

Recognition Begins in Private

The first time you acknowledge the contributions of a new staff member, do it in private. Take them into your office or somewhere else, out of sight and earshot of co-workers.

The new employee is not someone you know well. You don't know how he feels about recognition—particularly public recognition.

Express your appreciation. Describe what you saw the newcomer do well and how you feel about it. Explain how what the newcomer did is **Relevant** to the organization's values and goals.

Then observe how the newcomer reacts to recognition. Ask questions: "How do you feel about recognition? How do you prefer to be recognized when you do your job well?"

Talk about the importance of recognition in your organization. Introduce the concept of peer recognition. Ask if there is a co-worker who has helped during the newcomer's first few days. How could the newcomer express appreciation?

The Principal's Oval Office

In a conversation with a principal a few years ago, he expressed frustration that his office was perceived as the place where people only go to be disciplined. He had a plan to change that perception. Modelling the practice of U.S. presidents who invite members of championship sports teams to the Oval Office, he began to invite students to his office to congratulate them for their academic and athletic successes.

Certainly, when deserved, students and staff were still summoned to hear his displeasure with their performances, but the principal's office had also become a place to which people were invited to be congratulated and recognized.

Through his actions, this educational leader was breaking down stereotypes about being called to the office. Managers elsewhere can also change how their office is perceived. If it is always "reprimand-in-private-and-praise-in-public," co-workers perceive that anyone who enters the office is there to be disciplined. They may not know why, but they will speculate—potentially-harmful speculation that they often share with others.

However, once they learn that these visits may be occasions for someone to be recognized, a degree of uncertainty enters the workplace. Staff members can no longer predict what is going to happen. Was Joanne called to the office because she did wrong—or because she did right? Only Joanne and her manager know, and they aren't talking. Nor should they. It's no one else's business. What happens in the manager's office stays in the manager's office, unless the staff member decides to share.

Sure, always reprimand in private—never in public. But when acknowledging staff members' contributions and achievements, recognize in public some of the time and recognize in private at other times. As a rule, anything that confuses staff should be avoided. The exception may be when it comes to co-workers knowing that other staff members are meeting with the manager. Staff–and students–don't need to know why a colleague is called to the principal's office.

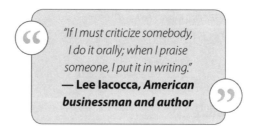

"If I must criticize somebody, I do it orally; when I praise someone, I put it in writing."
— Lee Iacocca, *American businessman and author*

Chapter 19
One Happy Winner...
Many Disappointed Losers

A few years ago, when it was challenge to recruit and retain staff, the management of a fast-food restaurant hit upon what it believed was the magic bullet—hold a contest. The rules were simple: apply for a job, get hired, and don't quit. Everyone who was still working for the company on July 1 was entered in a draw and eligible for the big prize, a trip for two to an all-inclusive Mexican resort.

I don't know how this experiment in staff recruitment and retention turned out, but I do know one thing. The company never repeated this attraction/retention exercise. Based on this fact, I can imagine a likely scenario.

As a recruitment tool, the contest worked. Attracted by the promise of a winter holiday in the sun, many applied and many were hired. Most shifts were fully staffed. The plan was working.

Not wishing to miss out on the possibility of a Mexican vacation, most staff continued with the company in the months and weeks leading up to the draw date. The number of resignations was down. The retention rate was up. The managers were delighted. These were the results they wanted.

Then the contest ended. One name was drawn from among those of all the staff members. This employee and a friend were on their way to Mexico. And for all the other loyal employees? Nothing! There could only be one winner. Which made everyone else a loser.

What happened next was something that the managers hadn't anticipated in their planning. Almost immediately, some of those who had only stayed around in hope of winning a Mexican vacation, quit. Over the next weeks, others followed suit.

The management was disappointed and confused. Turnover was more of a problem now than it had ever been before the contest. July was a record-breaking month: the most resignations in a single month. This wasn't the way things were supposed to work out.

Months later, the winner claimed her prize. She and a companion jetted off to the Mexican Rivera for a week of fun and sun at the company's expense. Back home, the turnover rate settled back to what it had been before the contest. Recruiting new staff was still a challenge. Staff retention was still a problem. The managers, who once had been so pleased with the results of their attraction/retention program, now weren't nearly as happy.

And there was one more surprise in store for the managers. Within days of returning from Mexico, the winner did what she had been planning to do for weeks. She quit!

This was now a very unhappy group of managers who had learned a painful lesson. As a way to motivate staff to do what managers want them to do, contests don't work. The promise of potential prizes may work initially, as was the case with the fast-food restaurant, but contests have no long-term benefit.

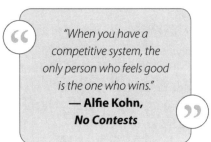

"When you have a competitive system, the only person who feels good is the one who wins."
— **Alfie Kohn,**
No Contests

Once it's over, it's over. The losers—and there are many of them—have nothing to show for performing up to expectations. They ask, "Why bother?"

A Workplace is Not a Casino

Most of us have participated in games of chance. We play bingo or purchase lottery tickets. We drop coins into slot machines or visit blackjack tables.

Workplace contests are a different game of chance. When it comes to buying a raffle ticket, individuals have a choice. While dreaming of the big win, the individual understands that the odds are against his winning. He accepts that he is likely to lose. Knowing this, he still makes the "investment" decision. He chooses to lose if the gambling gods don't smile upon him that day.

The employee whose reward for doing her job well is being entered in a draw for the big prize does not have a similar choice. She has been entered into the lottery whether she wants to experience the stress of waiting for her name to be called or not.

Being recognized for doing the job well may make a person feel like a winner, but contests produce more losers than winners. In the same instant as the winner is announced, a roomful of winners, whose names were entered into the draw by virtue of having performed well, becomes a gathering of losers. Contests produce too few winners and too many losers. Individuals who are made to feel like losers are unlikely to be motivated to produce winning performances. This is not the formula for creating productive teams or a successful organization.

"People who feel good about themselves produce good results."
— Ken Blanchard & Spenser Johnson, *The One Minute Manager*

Losing is disappointing, especially when the prize is something that people actually wanted to win.

Why Do Companies Do This?

Those who inflict the damage of a draw into a recognition program are likely well-intentioned managers who want to do something to recognize staff for their efforts. But what? Their answer: a contest with big prizes (vacation trips, big-screen TVs, a cash prize). Knowing that all the employees can become eligible for the prize by doing what is expected of them makes them feel they are doing something to motivate and recognize staff.

Unfortunately, they understand neither the value and power of day-to-day recognition nor the damage that contests cause. The acknowledgement from direct supervisors or co-workers is what people value and remember. Creating a bunch of losers by selecting one winner is likely to diminish the good memories that come from being recognized.

There are other unexpected and undesirable outcomes of contests other than producing a few winners and many losers. Some losers feel irrational resentment toward the winner. They believe that the winner somehow controlled the outcome. Even when the draw was obviously fair, conducted before all the potential winners, some losers feel anger toward those in leadership positions. They may believe that managers played favourites, allowing certain people to win.

There are other inequities inherent in this approach. Some contests allow for multiple entries. Every time a person is recognized, her name is added to the draw. It's like playing several bingo cards at once; your chances of winning are improved every time you are recognized. But it only takes one ticket to win. A person who was recognized only once—and on that occasion for a relatively minor contribution—may have his name drawn, while top performers whose names were entered several times are left to applaud the prize winner politely.

Some may criticize me for making such a big deal about draws creating more losers than winners. They would argue that the prize isn't important. It is all about the recognition that staff receive from knowing that someone has submitted their names.

I agree. Being told you are doing a good job by someone who matters to you is important. That being the case, why bother with the draw? What value is there in awarding a big prize to one staff member chosen from among all those who had been recognized earlier? Why create a bunch of losers when you already had a team of winners?

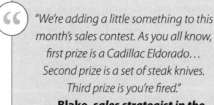

"We're adding a little something to this month's sales contest. As you all know, first prize is a Cadillac Eldorado... Second prize is a set of steak knives. Third prize is you're fired."
— Blake, *sales strategist in the movie Glengarry Glen Ross*

Chapter 20
Funerals for the Living

> **Question:** What is the difference between funerals and retirement parties?
> **Answer:** At one, the guest of honour is usually vertical; at the other, horizontal.

A few days after U.S. Senator Edward Kennedy was diagnosed with brain cancer in May 2008, a panel discussed his place in American political history on NBC's *Meet the Press*. The conversation focused on the tributes from political allies and foes alike, for Kennedy's contributions during nearly five decades in Washington. This prompted panellist and presidential historian Doris Kearns Goodwin to observe: "Boy, how lucky that he has been able to hear this. Hopefully he will live for 10 more years, but he has heard these wonderful remarks before he died."

I was shocked by these comments. How insensitive to the senator and his family!

> *"They say such nice things about people at their funerals that it makes me sad that to realize that I'm going to miss mine by just a few days."*
> **— Garrison Keillor, *American humourist and broadcaster***

Later, having reflected on the discussion, I came to understand the thought underlying the comments. Too often, family members, friends and colleagues die with many words that others wished to say left unsaid. Attend a few funerals and you are sure to hear someone say, "There are so many things I wish I had said to him while he was still alive."

Eulogies are filled with words never spoken when the person was still alive. Eulogists praise the deceased for his contributions to business, community and his family.

What a shame that the subject of these positive words is not alive to hear them. What would it have meant to him to have heard them when he was alive? What difference would that have made to his self-esteem or how he had lived his life?

Leaving one's work life behind is similar in some ways to dying. Both represent an end. Retirement even has its equivalent of funerals—retirement parties. The main difference is that at these funerals for the living, the guest of honour is sitting comfortably in a chair rather than resting in a coffin or urn.

Now that her work life has ended, the retiree is hearing how much her contributions were appreciated and how much she will be missed. These are the words that were left unsaid during her work life. What a waste! They should have been said earlier—and often.

In a conversation shortly after her retirement dinner, one top performer observed, "If I had heard some of those things earlier, I might have delayed my retirement." Watching how her former employer struggled to find a suitable replacement, it is unfortunate that the leaders in the organization had not spoken words of appreciation sooner. Knowing that she was valued, this employee might have stayed longer, providing time for effective succession planning.

"The best way to get praise is to die."
— Italian proverb

How You Say Goodbye is Important

There are two audiences for retirement events. The first is obvious—the retiree and his family. The second may be less obvious, but is just as important. The staff who remain observe how retirees are treated and remembered. They pay attention when the organization's leaders treat those who are retiring with respect and dignity, and honour the retirees' memories.

They also see when organizations appear intent on erasing any evidence that the retiree ever worked there. Executives seem threatened by the memories of former staff. Once the retirement event is over, the retiree's contributions are never again mentioned. In this way, today's business leaders are following a tradition that dates back to ancient times. Thousands of years ago in Egypt, each pharaoh would eradicate the record of his predecessor. Temple inscriptions were defaced. Monuments destroyed.

Even today, changes in governments are followed by efforts to remove any vestige of the previous rulers and to undo what they had done. This was illustrated once to a group of American, Australian and Canadian tourists crowded around a local guide in one of Prague's many squares. Lenka pointed to a nearby statue.

"That is Thomas Masaryk, the first president of Czechoslovakia," she said. "We never learned anything about him while we were at school. His name was never mentioned during communist times."

The fall of the former USSR was followed by the removal of portraits of the former communist leaders. The city of Leningrad once more became Saint Petersburg. As the American-led coalition moved into Baghdad in 2003, statues of Sadam Hussein were toppled.

Once a Team Member, Always a Team Member

Some sports teams have a simple way of honouring former players that any organization could adopt. Whenever a player leaves the team, whether through a trade, to free agency or retirement, the nameplate that marked his dressing room stall is removed and added to a place of honour in the dressing room, joining those of every other player who was part of the team since this tradition was introduced.

Why not do something similar in your organization? Display the nameplates or name tags of departed staff members as a way of honouring them for their contributions and achievements.

A message is sent to current employees by how departing staff are treated. When retirees are honoured and treated with respect and dignity, the remaining staff expects to be treated in similar fashion when their time comes, as well as during the remaining years of their work lives. Knowing that they will be treated well, staff may commit to creating memories that will be worth remembering.

"Always go to other people's funerals, otherwise they won't go to yours."
— **Yogi Berra, *former baseball player and manager***

DIY RECOGNITION RESEARCH:
The Eulogy

What you will need for this research project:
A pen and paper

Research Process:
1. Think how you would like to be remembered by your staff and co-workers.
2. Write a list of the words and phrases that you would like staff members to use if asked to write your eulogy.
3. Ask yourself, "Are these the words they would use?"

Implications for the Workplace:
If you feel staff would not use the words and phrases on your list, why not? What could you do to change list?

Hint: People will work hard for supervisors who they see as caring, respectful, good listeners, appreciative and honest.

Chapter 21
Hug People, Not Your Computer

I had an appointment at a client's office first thing on a Tuesday morning following a holiday weekend. When I arrived, several staff members were gathered in the reception area. While waiting for my meeting, I overheard staff members as they entertained each other with tales of their weekend adventures or previewed the shortened workweek that lay ahead.

Suddenly, the area became quiet. Everyone turned and watched as a figure appeared and quickly passed through the general office. It was George, the department head, who looked neither right nor left as he crossed the room, his eyes remaining fixed on the doorway to his private office. He appeared oblivious to the presence of his staff. He spoke to no one.

Once safely in his office, George slipped behind his desk, sat down and swivelled in his chair to face his computer screen. He remained in that position for the next 45 minutes, reading emails, responding to some.

Those who worked for George would describe this as a typical start to his workday. When he arrived each morning, he seemed more focused on renewing his relationship with his computer than with his staff.

"The best minute spent is one I invest in people."
— Ken Blanchard & Spenser Johnson,
The One Minute Manager

Except for occasional breaks to refill his coffee cup or visit the washroom, George never seemed to leave his office. His eyes remained fixed on the screen with his fingers poised over the keyboard—reading and composing email messages, visiting websites and preparing reports.

As this reception-area drama was unfolding, I mentally compared what I was witnessing to the opening credits of TV's *Barney Miller*. Over the course of its eight seasons (1974 – 1982), the series had at least three different opening sequences. In one version, the energetic New York police captain played by Hal Linden walks toward his precinct building. Several uniformed officers are standing on the street and the stairs leading into the building. As he passes, Barney smiles and greets them. He stops to share a joke with one.

When the venue was changed in other seasons to the squad room, Barney's behaviour didn't change, just more of the same—smiling, friendly greetings, brief conversations with the detectives.

Given a choice, which boss would you prefer—George or Barney? Most staff members would likely choose Barney, although many of them end up with someone like George.

The Gentleman of Shalott

There are thousands of managers similar to George in thousands of other departments of thousands of other organizations. These are men and women who seldom venture beyond the sanctuary of their offices. They live in self-imposed isolation, destined to observe life only as reflected on a computer screen—the modern day equivalent of the mirror through which the Lady of Shalott observed the road leading to Camelot.

> *And moving thro' a mirror clear*
> *That hangs before her all the year,*
> *Shadows of the world appear.*
> *There she sees the highway near*
> *Winding down to Camelot.*
> **— Alfred, Lord Tennyson**

She was cursed to remain in her island castle, weaving a magic web and never looking out on the world directly. One day, she sees Sir Lancelot's reflection as he rides pass. She can no longer remain in confinement. She leaves her castle, boards a boat and begins to float towards Camelot. Alas, she dies before reaching her destination.

Certainly, technology has a place in today's workplace. The Internet, email and other applications have put more knowledge at our fingertips, enhanced the distribution of information and made us more efficient.

Technology can also have a darker side. It can create distance between managers and staff. Less face-to-face communication reduces the importance of interpersonal skills. Rather than interacting and building relationships with staff, managers are able to hide behind a barrier of email and voice mail in the name of communication efficiency.

Those who avoid interaction with staff are often uncomfortable providing feedback, whether negative or positive. When it comes to acknowledging staff, these managers embrace the impersonal nature of formal recognition. It works

"The more high technology around us, the more the need for the human touch."
— **John Naisbitt,** ***Megatrends***

for them. But staff recognition is not about them. It's about those who are being recognized and what recognition is **Appropriate** for them. When they contribute to the success of the organization, staff members deserve to be recognized—in a way they prefer to be recognized. The type of recognition that many staff members desire is informal and face-to-face.

Workers see managers as potent sources of recognition, but only if that recognition is **Genuine.** The more managers are present, and the better staff members know and respect them, the more believable they are when they recognize staff for a job well done.

At Least 4 Ways Technology Can Serve Recognition

Technology doesn't have to be a barrier to recognition. It can be part of a manager's recognition tool kit. Here are a few suggestions for using technology when recognizing staff:

1. Send carefully selected e-cards—ones that reflect individual staff members' interests and personality. E-cards are available for free or at low cost from online suppliers (visit www.GREATstaffrecognition.com/resources for sources for e-cards). Use the message option to personalize the cards.

2. Create a blog in which you describe what you saw individuals do well as you "managed by walking around," and how you feel about what you saw.

3. Email congratulations for a staff member's achievements or thanks for a job well done—especially when distance makes face-to-face appreciation impossible. Occasionally, copy the individual's supervisor (if it's not you), or your supervisor.

4. Leave a message of appreciation on a staff member's voice mail, either at home or at work.

Managers who are seldom seen become irrelevant to staff members. When they do appear, they are viewed with fear and suspicion. "You only show up when someone is trouble," one teacher observed during a surprisingly candid conversation with an assistant superintendent during one of his infrequent visits to her school. It is hard to trust someone you seldom see.

When people work for managers who only show up for high-profile public recognition events and seldom provide informal, one-on-one recognition, they are not satisfied with the recognition they receive. Most staff members perceive the recognition that these managers provide as failing the critical test of being **Genuine.**

Do you have any grandchildren?

At a staff luncheon, a senior manager found himself seated next to one of his supervisors. In an attempt to initiate a non work-related conversation, he began with a question.

"Sharon, do you have any grandchildren?"

Yes, she replied. She had three, each of whom she described briefly.

The next day, Sharon admitted to a friend that she had momentarily considered another response. "Of course, I do. Whose photos do you think I have on my desk? But then again, how would you know about those? You've never been in my office."

The significance of Sharon's unspoken response? Her office was located just two doors from that of her manager, but he never went there. When he had something to say to her, he sent Sharon an email.

Most companies proclaim that, "Our people are our greatest asset," but the actions of managers and supervisors don't always match their words. Managers who believe this adage do treat staff as the most important people in the world. They understand that these are the people who keep them in business. They talk with them. They listen. They show interest in them and what they do. They provide support and recognize people for their successes.

 "A desk is a dangerous place from which to view the world."
— John le Carre, *British author*

Successful leaders are those who leave the security of their offices. They are driven to get out there where the action is. They spend time with their staff.

They understand that staff will treat customers in the same way as they are treated. Staff who are ignored are more likely to ignore customers. Staff who feel cared for are more likely to care for customers.

I feel that one can judge an organization and predict the quality of service experiences by observing the interaction between staff and supervisors. The more positive the interaction, as judged by the number of smiles and the frequency of laughter, the more positive our service experience is likely to be.

Applying "Management By Walking Around" Principles

In the 1980s, author and management consultant Tom Peters and others popularized the concept of management by walking—or wandering—around. Stripped down to its essentials, MBWA encourages managers to get out of the offices regularly to keep in touch with staff and customers, through informal visits and conversations with individuals.

MBWA is successful when those practising the concept understand why they are leaving their offices. They have a purpose. Without this, MBWA is of value to no one. It's a waste of the manager's time and leaves staff confused. A somewhat cynical observer once remarked that the way one manager practised MBWA might best be described as MBWA-AIL—managing by wandering around *as if lost*. The manager didn't understand why he had left his office. For other managers, MBWA fails when their purpose is to be to find fault or micromanage.

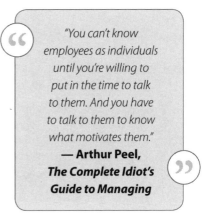

"You can't know employees as individuals until you're willing to put in the time to talk to them. And you have to talk to them to know what motivates them."
— **Arthur Peel,**
The Complete Idiot's Guide to Managing

MBWA works best when managers are there to observe, learn and discover successful performers. Effective MBWA managers believe that they can learn from those who are closest to the customers and understand their needs. If asked, most staff members could suggest ways to serve customers better or how to save money, increase productivity or improve efficiency.

These are not suggestions that staff will offer to managers who never leave their offices or who are perceived as not caring about what the staff is thinking.

MBWA also provides opportunities for managers to observe employees doing their jobs and provide **Timely,** on-the-spot recognition. What they see can also provide the basis for stories for success for later use, such as:

- When recognizing the staff member in front of co-workers
- During orientation of new staff
- On occasions of more formal recognition

Recognizing individuals for specific actions is a challenge. It is easy to be caught up in the big picture. Supervisors and managers see the outcomes, reflected in the number of widgets produced, student scores on exams, or sales figures. What they can miss are the small contributions and struggles that lead to these results. To be able to provide **Explicit** feedback related to day-to-day performance requires personal contact. It means knowing employees individually, and meeting with them from time to time to discuss their contributions and how what they do is **Relevant** to the bigger picture.

"If you wait for people to come to you, you'll only get small problems. You must go and find them. The big problems are where people don't realize they have one in the first place."
— W. Edwards Deming,
American author and consultant

DIY RECOGNITION RESEARCH: A Day's Worth of Positives

What you will need to conduct this research:
Nothing

Research Process:
Set a goal to provide positive feedback, and only positive feedback, for a full day. No negative feedback at all.

At the end of the day, reflect on the experience:
Were you successful? Were you able to do it—just say positive things all day long? How difficult was this to do? How did others respond?

Implications for the Workplace:
For most of us, this would be a difficult challenge. It seems that we are hard-wired to focus on the negative. Those of us who grew up in the Judeo-Christian tradition recall that most of the Ten Commandments begin, "Thou shall not." At work, we are surrounded by policies and procedures that tell us what we can't do ("I'm sorry, but that's against company policy.") We just feel that things that go wrong deserve most of our attention. Good things will look after themselves.

Hint: For centuries, mothers have been advising their children, "If you can't say anything nice, don't say anything at all." It's good advice to keep in mind—at home or at work.

Chapter 22
Teams, Stars and Recognition

Outside Rexall Place, the home of the National Hockey League's Edmonton Oilers, there is a statue of Wayne Gretzky. The hockey superstar triumphantly holds the Stanley Cup above his head.

While this monument commemorates the Great One's legendary career, it also reminds fans of the Oilers' glory years of the 1980s, when the team won five championships in just seven years.

Teams that win championships are comprised of individuals who are selected for their talents and brought together to achieve a specific goal. Each player brings different skills to the team, which means that each one contributes in different ways. Some contribute more, as Gretzky and other future Hall-of-Famers did. But there were times when others—the "role players" in hockey jargon—were the most productive players on the ice.

When the Oilers won their championships, all the players shared those moments of glory. As soon as the buzzer signaled the end of the final playoff game, players on the bench leaped over the boards to join those already on the ice. The team celebration had begun.

After a few minutes, the players gathered round for the presentation of the championship trophy, after which

"The one nice thing about sports is that they prove men do have emotions and are not afraid to show them."
— Jane O'Reilly,
The Girl I Left Behind

the celebration resumed. The ceremony over, each athlete had his moment with the Stanley Cup. Every player hoisted the Cup over his head and went for a short skate with the Cup, before passing the trophy on to a colleague.

The team that won together celebrated together.

During the cliché-filled post-game interviews in any sport, players and coaches credit the victory to "team effort." They often remark that, "Everyone parked his ego at the door. Every player gave 110 per cent all season."

This is the spirit of teamwork: everyone contributing to the team achieving its goals.

Most of us are familiar with the concept of teamwork in non-sports environments. Surveys show that most organizations describe themselves as embracing the team concept. As in sports, the world of business has its own team-inspired clichés:

"Together Everyone Achieves More."
"There's no I in Team, but without U there is no success."

In many ways, the team concept makes sense in non-sporting environments. Individuals bring a diversity of skills, knowledge and resources from which the entire team can benefit:

- Team members can learn from each other.
- Leadership of teams is often shared, which means that the wisdom of many—not just that of one boss—can guide the team's efforts.
- Teams often solve problems more successfully than one person working in isolation does.
- Many people feel energized by being part of a team. There is a sense of belonging. Being part of a team can contribute to meeting the social aspect of Abraham's Maslow's hierarchy of needs.
- Teams have synergy. They are able to utilize the different expertise, experience and personalities of their members.

"One thing I believe to the fullest is that if you think and achieve as a team, the individual accolades will take care of themselves. Talent wins games, but teamwork and intelligence win championships."
— Michael Jordon, *I Can't Accept Not Trying*

- Team members can work together to improve processes and to reduce costs and waste.
- Teams have a common sense of direction. Work can be completed more efficiently when everyone understands the team's goals.

Like sports teams, work teams should celebrate their successes—increasing productivity, meeting goals, completing projects. Everyone who contributed should be part of the celebration of the team's achievement. Including everyone reinforces the value of the team and helps create a sense of belonging and team cohesiveness.

While team recognition is important, it does not replace the need for individual recognition. One complements the other. While people can achieve much as a team, each member is an individual who wants feedback and to know that he is seen and valued as an individual, not simply just one part of a group working toward a common goal.

To deny individuals the recognition they yearn for and deserve due to a commitment to team recognition is to leave people only partly recognized. While their contributions may be no more or less valuable than those of their colleagues, each person contributes differently, reflecting differences in knowledge, experience, skills and commitment. Each person is selected for the team based on the individual strengths he will bring to the group, which is one of the greatest values of work teams. These individual contributions made by team members should be celebrated.

Some supervisors are reluctant to recognize individuals, fearing that by doing so they will damage the spirit of teamwork. Recognizing individuals may be seen as favouritism. Or supervisors might believe that individual recognition may introduce competitiveness to the workplace that is contrary to the spirit of teamwork. Team members may become jealous or resentful of co-workers who have been recognized. Feelings may be hurt.

"Above all for those upon whose smile and well being our own happiness depends, and also for those countless unknown souls with whose fate we are connected by a bond of sympathy. Many times a day I realize how much my own outer and inner life is built upon the labours of my fellow man, both living and dead, and how earnestly I must exert myself in order to give in return as much as I have received."
— Albert Einstein, *physicist*

At Least 12 Ways to Recognize Team Success

1. Attend the first meeting of a project team to express your appreciation that they are willing to undertake the task and your confidence in their ability to complete it successfully.

2. When submitting a report that was produced by a team, list all those who contributed.

3. Invite everyone to a celebratory lunch or dinner, or host a pizza lunch or barbeque in the company parking lot at the successful conclusion of a project.

4. Provide the team with a budget and invite it to design its own celebration.

5. Schedule a team outing—a movie, sporting event or concert.

6. Involve team members in planning for celebrations as milestones are reached, rather than always waiting until the project has been completed.

7. Provide the team with greater authority to direct its own work and make budget decisions.

8. Invite the team to select its own projects and set its own goals.

9. Schedule a teamwork day when teams from different departments can show off what can be accomplished through teamwork.

10. If the team wins an award, allow each member to "own" it for a day or week, during which time they can display it in their work areas or take it home to share with the family. Awards are not won just to gather dust on a shelf in the corporate office. (Each member of the NHL's championship team is given the Stanley Cup for a day, during which time many players take it back to where they grew up or where they first played hockey to show it off to the hometown fans.)

11. At the successful conclusion of a project, present the team with a collage that is comprised of mementos of their journey…photos of them at work, related newspaper or newsletter articles, and other items that reflect what they had to do to succeed.

12. Set aside a spot to display memos, photographs and other items that demonstrate the progress your staff is making on a major project. Be sure to include words of appreciation and encouragement.

Team Building vs. Team Recognition

Some of what is passed off as team recognition is actually team building. These are activities that are meant to develop cohesiveness by fostering trust and communication among team members to improve team performance. Team recognition is different because it involves identifying and praising behaviours that help the team reach its goals.

Whether team building or team recognition, the activities may be similar but the purposes are different:

- Inviting team members to get to know each other better while sharing a meal is team building. Inviting people to meet for dinner to celebrate reaching this quarter's production target is team recognition.
- Going golfing with co-workers to improve morale is team building. Taking the team to a golf course to mark the end of a project is team recognition.
- Asking each person to identify his strengths and interests is team building. Describing how team members combined their strengths to complete a task ahead of schedule is team recognition.

These are valid concerns, but ones that can be overcome by combining both team and individual recognition. Team recognition can lead to individual recognition. Begin by describing what the team achieved, followed by identification of team members' contributions.

On effective teams, members care about each other. They understand that there will be times when some people contribute more than others and should be recognized for this.

Consider again the Edmonton Oilers of the 1980s. In addition to Gretzky, the team included several other future Hall-of-Famers, such as Mark Messier, Grant Fuhr, Jari Kurri, Glenn Anderson and Paul Coffey. Their names are displayed on banners above the ice at Rexall Place—their sweater

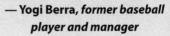

"When you're part of a team, you stand up for your teammates. Your loyalty is to them. You protect them through good and bad, because they'd do the same for you."
— **Yogi Berra, *former baseball player and manager***

numbers are retired. No future Oiler will ever wear these numbers on their jerseys. Most of them won individual league awards and each played in several all-star games.

But there were others on the Oilers teams who are less well remembered today—Charlie Huddy, Dave Hunter, Dave Semenko, Randy Gregg, Kent Nilsson and Esa Tikkanen. Each of these role players contributed to the Oilers becoming a hockey dynasty.

> "Individual commitment to a group effort—that is what makes a team work, a company work, a society work, a civilization work."
> — **Vince Lombardi, legendary football coach**

When role players saw their more-talented colleagues singled out for individual recognition, they celebrated their success. When one of these less-talented players had a particularly outstanding game and was rewarded by being named as one of the game's three stars, their higher-profile teammates celebrated their success.

Team Recognition Should be GREAT

The acronym **GREAT,** which is so important for providing meaningful individual recognition, can also be applied to team recognition. Doing so will lead to discoveries of why recognition cannot be limited to the team only. Team recognition and individual recognition should complement each other.

Genuine – Before providing recognition ask, "Do all team members deserve to be treated equally?" Avoid generalization such as, "You all did a great job," when everyone knows it would be more truthful to refer to "most" or "some" as doing a great job. Focus on what the team achieved collectively. "As a team, you accomplished a great deal…"

Relevant – What is being recognized should relate to why the team was established and how it contributes to fulfilling the organization's mission and reaching its goals.

Explicit – The more specific you are about what the team achieved, the more you will find that you are describing the contributions of individuals.

Appropriate – The larger the team, the more difficult it becomes to find ways to recognize that match everyone's recognition preferences. A colleague recalls once working for a company that had several football season tickets that were used for recognition purposes. Even though she doesn't understand or like football, she felt obliged to attend when she was given tickets. Because all the seats were together, it would have been obvious if she had passed the tickets on to a friend who was a football fan or simply stayed away. The gesture of appreciation that some of her co-workers may have valued was meaningless to her.

Timely – To be most meaningful, recognition must be delivered as soon after the team achieves its goals as possible. As the co-ordination of several schedules is difficult, it may be best to celebrate team success during normal working time.

At Least 6 Ways to Transition from a Team-Only Recognition Workplace to One With More Individual Recognition

In some organizations where teamwork is valued, recognition efforts are designed to recognize the contribution of the team as a whole, not its individual members. How do supervisors in organizations that emphasize teamwork make the transition to providing more individual recognition and maintain a sense of fairness and teamwork? Here are a few suggestions:

1. On a person's employment anniversary, spend time with that individual. Congratulate and thank her for completing another year with your organization before highlighting two or three recent contributions or achievements that she made. Say thank you, and end the conversation by wishing the employee success during the next year.

2. Birthdays are often celebrated in the workplace. Join the celebration by saying a few words about the individual. Begin with birthday wishes. Then take advantage of the opportunity to highlight one or two things that the birthday boy has done recently that benefited the organization or helped co-workers.

3. Begin in private. Over the course of a few days, invite each team member into your office for a brief conversation. Ask them about their work. What is going well? Listen and focus on what they say. Explain why you agree with their assessments and add your words of praise. Provide your own examples of something they did that you appreciated.

4. Put it in writing. Leave a handwritten note on each employee's desk. Describe one thing that individual did recently that you appreciate. Ensure that what is described is different for each person. They may compare notes or they may pin your words to a bulletin board in their work area where others will see them.

5. Encourage peer recognition. A sign of a high-performing team is when members acknowledge co-workers for their contributions.

6. Focus on what the individual did well when recognizing her in the presence of other team members. Avoid the teamwork-destroying practice of comparing her performance to that of others, by using phrases such as "the best worker in our department."

Chapter 23
How Green is Staff Recognition?

There was a question I thought about repeatedly following the 2008 Recognition Professionals International (RPI) conference in Newport Beach, California. Is staff recognition environmentally unfriendly?

At the registration desk, we were told that the conference was "going green." Many of the presentation handouts were on a USB flash drive. Attendees were encouraged to refill the plastic water bottles found in their conference bags. The bottles and bags were made from recycled materials. Provisions were made on-site to recycle paper and drink bottles. We were asked to return name-badge holders at the end of the conference for reuse. Rather than being presented with gifts that they might not need or use, speakers were told that 15 trees would be planted on their behalf in the nearby San Diego area devastated by wildfires only a few months earlier.

RPI invited attendees to submit suggestions to make future conferences even greener. These suggestions were entered into a draw for travel mugs that were awarded throughout the conference.

During the conference, there was a day-long trade show where suppliers displayed their wares—plaques, certificates, trophies, paperweights, boxed pen sets, clocks, desk caddies, mugs, lapel pins. The list could go on forever. Supplying recognition trinkets is big business. Bob Nelson, the author of several best-selling books, including *1001 Ways to Reward Employees* and *The 1001 Rewards & Recognition Fieldbook* estimates that $27 billion is spent annually on recognition merchandise.

One imagines that those who spend this money are giving what they purchase to their staff to convey messages of appreciation for what they do and what they achieve.

But then what? What happens to this stuff after it has been presented? Certainly, some plaques will be displayed on the walls of the recipients' offices or homes. A few trophies will adorn bookcase shelves. Some employees will sip their morning coffee from company mugs.

But not all the plaques, trophies, and mugs will be treasured in the same way. After gathering dust for a few weeks or months, they will be discarded. Recipients do not value what was given to them because what was given was not **Appropriate** for the recipient.

Recently, an acquaintance unintentionally illustrated this point. She showed me a set of glasses etched with her employer's logo that she—and every other employee—had received to mark a milestone in the company's development.

"I would really like to have more of these," she told me. "They are really expensive glasses, but most people don't know that. I am sure I'll be able to buy more at garage sales next summer."

While some may recycle unwanted trinkets through garage sales or donations to charities, many others will simply discard them with the household trash. There is not much of a resale market for unwanted plaques and trophies. Up to 90 per cent of the money being spent on recognition trinkets is wasted. Many of these items are destined for landfills.

How does one avoid environmentally unfriendly staff-recognition practices? First, don't assume that, just because you like something, your staff will too. Get to know your employees. If gift giving is part of your recognition plan, ensure that what you give is **Appropriate**—something they will value and use. Or give gift cards that recipients can use to purchase something that they will actually use. Even better, stop relying on things to carry your messages of gratitude. Thank employees face-to-face, or send them a simple thank-you note.

At Least 8 Ways to Green Up Staff Recognition

1. Plant a tree to honour an employee or welcome a new staff member ("We can all watch the tree—and your career—grow.")
2. Recognize staff members who suggest ways to make your company greener.
3. Acknowledge staff that use public transportation to get to work. Reserve the best parking spots for those who car pool.
4. Present a staff member with a plant to green up his work area.
5. Present a reusable water bottle to a staff member who "helped us keep our heads above water" during a busy time.
6. Set up containers to collect drink containers for recycling. Invite the team to identify a charity to support with the money you receive when the containers are taken to the bottle depot.
7. Use e-cards to express appreciation. For a list of sources for e-cards, visit www.GREATstaffrecogniton.com/resources.
8. When organizing company recognition events, think green. What can be done to produce less garbage? Limit printed materials and print only what you need on recycled paper. Use recyclable and reusable items whenever possible. Select a venue based on its green plan. Send invitations via email.

Chapter 24
This Fat Lady Will Never Sing

One Thing Yogi Never Said

One of the 20th century's most-quoted men is also one of its most misquoted. Former baseball great Yogi Berra seemed to acknowledge this in the subtitle of his 1998 memoir, *The Yogi Book: I Really Didn't Say Everything I Said.*

"This was a comment I made when someone asked me about quotes that I didn't think I said. Then again, I might have said 'em, but you never know."

One of the most popular Yogi Berra misquotations describes a night at the opera: "It ain't over until the fat lady sings."

The quotation has actually been traced to two sportscasters who uttered it long before Yogi was alleged to have done so.

"Misquotations are the only quotations that are never misquoted."
— Hesketh Pearson,
British actor and writer

There are few actions that are more satisfying than taking a pen, and with a bold stroke, crossing out a now-completed task from your to-do list. It feels so good to know that something you needed to do is done!

Some managers and supervisors would prefer to approach staff recognition in the same fashion as completing a report, booking a hotel room, or ordering office supplies. Just another task to add to a to-do list, complete and cross off. Done! It's over. Time to move on to another task.

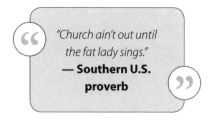

"Church ain't out until the fat lady sings."
— **Southern U.S. proverb**

Some recognition-related tasks do lend themselves to a do-it-once-and-it's-done approach:

- Taking your assistant for lunch during Administrative Professionals Week
- Handing out awards at the annual service banquet
- Showing your appreciation for everyone's contributions by hosting a staff picnic during the third week of June every year

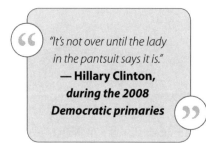

"It's not over until the lady in the pantsuit says it is."
— **Hillary Clinton, during the 2008 Democratic primaries**

Once completed, these events are done with until next year's appreciation week, service banquet or picnic. That's staff recognition looked after, so now it's on to some of those important tasks.

While this may be true for calendar-specific recognition events, the need to let staff know they are appreciated for what they do is never satisfied. Once a year is not enough.

By this point in the book, you know that I feel this type of once-a-year recognition breeds cynicism more than a sense of being appreciated. No single event or act of recognition is going to create a positive workplace where people feel valued for who they are and appreciated for what they do. They need to be cared for as individuals and recognized frequently by both supervisors and co-workers for their contributions and achievements. Some of this may come through formal recognition, but most will result from high-value, low-cost informal recognition.

Events and programs just don't cut it unless they exist within a culture of informal, day-to-day recognition that is **GREAT—Genuine** and at least one of the following: **Relevant, Explicit, Appropriate** or **Timely.**

And frequent!

This is not the type of thing that ever gets permanently crossed off a to-do list. Recognize a few staff today and still, the need to recognize staff pops up on tomorrow's to-do list. Maybe it will be different people who get recognized tomorrow, but the need to remind people that they are appreciated never goes away. The need is there every day.

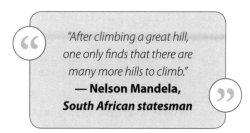

"After climbing a great hill, one only finds that there are many more hills to climb."
— Nelson Mandela, South African statesman

Providing Recognition Addicts with their Daily Fix

Staff recognition is a marathon, not a sprint. Actually, it is more like a series of marathons—one day after the next. Once you start, you won't be able to stop. Start recognizing staff and you will create addicts. Your staff will need their regular fix of appreciation. When you see how staff responds to the meaningful recognition, you will become addicted to it as well. You will want to feed their habit.

Recognition ain't ever going to be over!

Another reality of the never-ending nature of staff recognition is that you will never get recognition completely right nor will you be as good at recognizing staff as you could or would like to be.

Monitor how you recognize staff so you can make adjustments to provide ever more meaningful expressions of appreciation in the future. Monitoring can take different forms:

Observation – How is staff responding to the recognition they receive? How is staff morale? Has the frequency of peer recognition changed? How have staff turnover rates improved?

Discussion – Ask staff how they feel about recognition. Do they feel they are being thanked often enough? For the right reasons? In the right way?

Surveys – Invite staff to respond to questions and compare results with those from previous surveys (See Chapter 29, "Do You Know What Your Staff Thinks?" for tips on conducting your own staff surveys).

"Even if you're on the right track, you'll get run over if you just sit there."
— Mark Twain, American author

Self-Assessment – Conduct your own staff recognition post mortems regularly. After acknowledging someone for her contributions, pause to ask yourself:

- What about this act of gratitude went well?
- What did I do to make this recognition meaningful to the recipient?
- How did the recipient respond to the recognition?
- What could I have done differently?
- Have other forms of recognition worked better with this person in the past?
- Was the setting in which the recognition was delivered **Appropriate** for this employee?
- Did the recognition achieve the results I wanted?
- What did I learn from this recognition experience that I can apply when recognizing staff in the future?

Assessment Will Lead to Change and Improvement

From time to time, you will discover that changes are needed. Specific techniques may not be **Appropriate** for some staff. Even a technique that worked well with an individual in the past may now have become less meaningful. Eventually, being recognized in the same way, no matter how satisfying it once was, becomes boring for the recipient—and likely for the person doing the recognizing as well.

When the same technique is used too often, it comes to feel like just another in the list of employment benefits—life insurance, sick leave, extended health care, the boss buying lunch. It is expected. An entitlement. It ceases to be something special.

Recognizing staff in different ways can increase the impact of your expressions of gratitude. Variety makes recognition more memorable. Change for the sake of change is a way to keep recog-

> "*Every day you may make progress. Every step may be fruitful. Yet there will stretch out before you an ever-lengthening, ever-ascending, ever-improving path. You know you will never get to the end of the journey. But this, so far from discouraging, only adds to the joy and glory of the climb.*"
> — **Winston Churchill, former British prime minister**

nition fresh.

The best ways to recognize staff will evolve as the workforce changes. What worked well for a previous generation of workers may not be the best way to praise members of a younger workforce.

"We must always change, renew, rejuvenate ourselves; otherwise we harden."
— **Johann Wolfgang von Goethe,** *German writer*

Sometimes, the effectiveness of recognition practices is not just related to the changing face of the workforce. Recognition, especially via formal recognition programs, loses its energy over the years. No one may even remember why the program was introduced a couple of decades ago.

Even though a program may have lost its impact and isn't working as it once did, it can be difficult to allow it to quietly fade into history. There are always a few who are attached to the way staff have always been recognized and who don't want to let go. If protestations are too loud, this may mean that what initially had been introduced as a way of distinguishing good performance has evolved to a point where it is now considered an entitlement.

Make a clean break from from recognition practices of the past. Rather than simply dropping the program, you may need to end the practice with a celebration—hold a retirement party for the recognition program whose time has come.

Becoming a masterful recognizer takes time. Likely you will never be as good at recognizing staff as you could be, would want to be, or will need to be to meet the needs of all staff members to be acknowledged.

But you are committed to growing and improving your skills at acknowledging staff for their contributions and achievements. That's why you have read this, and other books and articles about staff recognition. You likely do a better job of recognizing staff today than you did a year ago. And a year from now, you will likely be better at staff recognition than you are right now.

Part of the never-ending nature of the task of staff recognition is a never-ending commitment to learn more about staff recognition and develop new skills and techniques. I am also committed to your growth. I encourage you to visit www.GREATstaffrecognition.com. Here you will find information that didn't fit into this book, new thinking about staff recognition, additional staff recognition tips, and information about products and services that will assist you to grow as someone who recognizes staff well.

While visiting this website, take time to describe your own successes when recognizing staff, pose questions about staff recognition and subscribe to *Briefly Noted,* a free, informative and thought-provoking email that I send out regularly. *Briefly Noted* will always include articles about staff recognition and high-value, low-cost tips and techniques that you can use to say thank you to those around you.

Stop waiting for the fat lady to sing. Just keep recognizing staff. This is a need that will never go away. She's never going to sing!

Excuses, Rationalizations and Cop-outs (Part III)

"They are doing just fine as things are now. Why rock the boat by introducing something new?"

Positive feedback encourages people in their work. Feedback motivates them to do more of what was recognized positively. Receiving and witnessing others receiving **Explicit** and **Relevant** recognition helps people understand what is expected of them.

When we give people a positive image of themselves, they tend to live up to it. Don't worry that we might accidentally give undeserved praise. When we make a statement about a person's effort, even if we have inadvertently exaggerated, we contribute to that person's positive self-image. She will be motivated to live up to the image that we appear to have.

When well-delivered, recognition can motivate staff to become more productive, and this is key to the organization's overall success.

"Around here, no news is good news. Everyone knows that I have high expectations. Don't meet them and you're history. Obviously, anyone who still has a job is doing a good job."

When it comes to people's employment, no news is definitely not good news. People want to know how they are doing and whether they are on the right track. The absence of feedback creates an information vacuum that is soon filled with rumour and speculation. People imagine what the missing feedback would be. Often, what they imagine is negative, creating stress and uncertainty. Worried workers are less

> *"I am suggesting to you the simple idea that people work harder and smarter if they find their work satisfying and know that it is appreciated."*
> **— Robert F. Six,**
> **former CEO,**
> **Continental Airlines**

productive than those who are motivated and confident that they are valued.

In a study conducted in the 1940s, and replicated several times since with similar results, Lawrence Lindahl discovered that what workers wanted most from their jobs is to be appreciated for the work they do and to feel "in" on things. Recognition helps satisfy both these wants.

Every time you recognize someone for what she did, you are sending a message about your expectations—what's important to you. Both the person being recognized and those who witness the recognition when it is done publicly, see what kind of behaviour is valued. They will be motivated to do more of whatever it is the recognition demonstrated that you want.

"I don't want to resort to bribery to get people to do what they already should be doing."

The Canadian Oxford Dictionary defines a bribe as "a sum of money or another reward offered or demanded in order to procure an…action or decision in favour of the giver." Quid pro quo. A payoff.

Uh…sounds a little the definition of a paycheque, doesn't it? Do an adequate job and you'll get paid at the end of the week. A paycheque is something employees will get as long as they are employed, whether they do their job well or not.

Recognition is different. It is a little extra that is bestowed on the worker only if she has done the job well. Unlike the expected paycheque, recognition is always somewhat unexpected. Even if recognition is common in the workplace, it doesn't have the certainty of a paycheque. Part of what makes recognition valuable is that there is an

"And it's that hunger for recognition that drives them to leave for other jobs—searching for greener pastures where they will feel needed and appreciated."
— Adrian Gostick & Chester Elton, *The 24-Carrot Manager*

element of surprise: how it's given; where it's given; by whom. Recognition is never as predictable as a paycheque…or any other bribe.

"The union won't let us do it."

Where did you get this idea? Does the collective agreement contain a clause prohibiting management from saying thank you to union members? Have you ever asked union leaders for their views on staff recognition?

When I asked the president of a union local whether this was a valid reason not to recognize staff, her first response was laughter. A member of the leadership of another union said he could think of no reason why supervisors should not recognize union members—or anyone else for that matter—for their contributions.

There are a few things to consider when recognizing staff in a unionized environment. Avoid using money as a recognition tool. It may get in the way of the compensation package negotiated into the collective agreement. This is not a big loss, as money itself is a poor motivator in most work situations. As in any workplace, it is important that recognition be delivered fairly. Recognition should be tied to actions that are **Relevant** to individual, on-the-job success and the organization's goals and values.

If you intend to increase the prominence of staff recognition, make the union aware of what you will be doing and why. Invite it to be part of both the planning and the implementation.

"You've got to keep after people if you want them to do well."

Yelling at people just doesn't work, especially not over time. Negative feedback may have a short-term impact of productivity, but it seldom lasts. Employees aren't naive. They will learn to keep their heads down, doing enough to avoid negative feedback. There is no motivation to go the extra mile, take risks or innovate. What they may be motivated to do, however, is search for a more positive work environment.

"What do you mean we never recognize them? Every Christmas we give them a turkey to show how much they are appreciated!"

In place of "give them a turkey," you could substitute, "invite them to a company picnic," "give them an annual bonus," or "celebrate their birthdays and service anniversaries."

These are all things that some managers and supervisors believe are recognition, but they aren't. Do it once, it is an expression of appreciation. Do it the next year, and it comes to be expected. And what is expected soon becomes an entitlement, along with other components of the income and benefits package.

The turkey isn't special anymore. Rather than being something that makes people feel valued and appreciated, the turkey becomes a catalyst for complaints.

"It's not as big as the one we got last year."
"Why do they only give us frozen turkeys?"
"Why can't they give us a fresh bird?"
"I hate turkey!"

"Too many people miss the silver lining because they're expecting gold."
— Maurice Setter, *author*

DIY RECOGNITION RESEARCH:
Doing It Poorly or Doing It Well

What you will need for this research project:
Paper and pencil, timing device

Research Process:
1. Draw a line down the middle of a paper.

What Staff Does Well	What Staff Does Poorly

2. Set the timer for two minutes. In two minutes, list as many things your staff does well as possible.
3. Reset the timer for two minutes. This time, list as many things as you can think of that your staff does poorly.
4. Analyze the lists:
   - Which list is longer?
   - Which list is more specific?
   - Which list was easier to complete?

Implications for the Workplace:
What is the focus of the feedback you provide—what staff does poorly or what they do well? Does the feedback you provide reflect the length of the two lists you created?

Hint: One writer estimated that staff members do their job correctly 95 per cent of the time, yet 85 per cent of the feedback they receive is negative. Doesn't seem right, does it?

Please note that this form is available online at:
www.GREATstaffrecognition.com/bookbonus/DIYforms
You have permission to print it for your use to conduct this recognition research.

SECTION FOUR
Moving Forward: How to Enhance Staff Recognition

Chapter 25
Be Led Not Into Temptation, Lest It Render Recognition Ineffective

As part of a review of a client's staff recognition practices, I contacted several other organizations to learn how they recognized staff. What could I learn from their practices that my client could use to enhance their staff recognition efforts?

Despite varying in size, location and business type, most organizations had one thing in common. With only a couple of exceptions, the people with whom I spoke began with a description of their service awards—the frequency with which staff were honoured, how they were honoured, and the time and resources that were consumed in preparing for a special event at which the recognition would be bestowed.

On another occasion, an executive who ran the local 150-person office of a national corporation invited me to lunch to discuss staff recognition. She explained that in response to the question, "How can we make this a better place to work?" staff had said they felt unappreciated. "Couldn't you let us know that we are doing a good job more often?" they asked.

Her solution was to create an employee-of-the-week program. Each week she solicited nominations from the staff. From those names she selected one person who became the employee-of-the-week and received a $50 gift card. The email that staff received announcing the name of the weekly winner also included a general thank you to everyone for their hard work.

"How's that working for you?" I asked.

"Fine. We've only been doing it for a few weeks and we get several suggestions each week," my dining partner replied. "It can be hard to choose just one person."

Fast forward a few weeks. Things aren't going so well. The nominations from staff have dried up. Coming up with someone to recognize each week has become difficult. Soon afterwards, the employee-of-the-week program was quietly discontinued.

In both these examples, those who were making decisions about staff recognition had fallen prey to some of the temptations that frequently victimize those who are new to staff recognition, or who are attempting to increase and improve how they recognize staff. Giving into any of these temptations has the potential to derail staff recognition efforts:

Temptation #1: Needing to "Go Big or Go Home"

For many runners, completing a marathon is the ultimate goal. Reaching this pinnacle of running does not occur overnight. No one ever decides one day to abandon a sedentary lifestyle to enter his first marathon the next day. Future marathoners begin with a series of smaller steps that eventually lead to a half marathon, and finally to the full 42.195 km.

Unlike runners who train for months to enter a marathon, some managers and supervisors believe they can move from sitting on the staff recognition sidelines to recognition superstars overnight. The only way they see to recognize staff is with the recognition equivalent of a marathon—a big event, with big gifts and awards, presented in public.

It doesn't work. This type of recognition is unsustainable. Too time consuming, too expensive and too ineffective. As with the future marathoner, mastering recognition works best when begun with small steps. By starting small and sustaining your efforts over time, you can build a culture of recognition within your organization.

Many couch potatoes become runners as a way to increase their physical activity—not to become marathoners. Running makes them feel better physically and emotionally. Most never run marathons or aspire to run one. They are content to go for a daily jog and maybe enter an occasional five or 10-km fun run.

The same can be true of those who abandon their staff recognition, couch-potato lifestyle. They–and more importantly, their staff–find satisfaction in small acts of gratitude to let staff know they are valued and that what they do is appreciated, supplemented by the occasional special event.

A key to staff recognition success is to commit to the process, understanding you are making a long-term commitment. One-time big recognition events are not the way to make staff feel appreciated.

Initial efforts to recognize staff should be simple and low-key. Once one begins to focus on recognizing staff, it becomes obvious that people deserve to be recognized for different things in different ways at different times. The message of appreciation must be repeated to become believable.

Temptation #2: Making a Covert Transition to More Recognition

Some potential recognizers are reluctant to talk to others about their desire to improve staff recognition. They may fear admitting that they have not recognized staff well or often enough in the past, or fear failing to do a better job in the future.

Part of getting started can be letting others know you plan to do a better job of recognizing staff. Meet with staff members, either individually or as a group to confess that you aren't acknowledging their contributions as well as you could. You feel that they are not hearing your expressions of appreciation as often as they deserve. Share your commitment to become better at expressing your appreciation. Invite them to offer advice and help plan for enhanced recognition.

Script to Introduce More Recognition

"Something that I don't do often or well enough is letting people know that I appreciate them for their good work. I want to get better at this, starting today, by letting you know that you did a good job of _____. I particularly like the way you _____ _____. This is the type of effort that we value around here, because it will help us meet our goals successfully."

Temptation #3: Beginning in Public

Sometimes public recognition seems meant more to impress an audience than to acknowledge the contributions and achievements of an individual. It demonstrates that the supervisor understands that recognition is important, and that she is doing something about it. Public recognition is important and valued by many people, but recognition delivered in private may be more meaningful. In private, the focus is on just one person.

Your staff recognition efforts will seem more **Genuine** if the first recognition employees receive is delivered in private. In the privacy of your office, it is clear that the gesture of appreciation is meant for the individual who is being acknowledged, not to impress others with what a great job you do of expressing appreciation.

Private recognition can be simple and low-key. Away from the eyes of others, you can monitor how the recipient responds to recognition. And the recipient is freed from having to respond in ways that an audience might expect.

Temptation #4: Recognizing Everyone at Once

Certainly everyone should be recognized. But not at the same time, or in the same way. Doing so appears like it was meant to save time–or make up for lost time–rather than to acknowledge specific achievement or accomplishments. There are times when the full team should be recognized for completing a project. But teams are made up of individuals, each of whom makes a unique contribution. While no one's contribution is necessarily more or less valuable than those of co-workers, each contribution is different and should be acknowledged differently.

Recognizing the contributions of individuals shows that you understand what each staff member does, which leaves the person feeling valued as an individual and motivated to repeat the behaviours that you notice and appreciate.

 "Nothing is more unequal than the equal treatment of unequals."
— Vince Lombardi, *former NFL coach*

Temptation #5: Attempting Too Many Techniques at Once

There are hundreds of ideas out there—at conferences, online and in books such as this one—suggesting how staff should be recognized. Ignore most of them. Focus on acknowledging staff in a few ways with which you are comfortable. As you become more confident in recognizing staff you can expand your repertoire and strive to recognize staff in ways that are most **Appropriate** for each individual.

 "I am only one, but still I am one. I cannot do everything, but I can still do something. I will not refuse to do the something I can do."
— Helen Keller, American author

Temptation #6: Believing the Excuses

I have begun workshops by asking, "What prevents managers or supervisors from recognizing staff more often?" I have heard more than 20 reasons for recognition inertia.

Don't believe any of them. They are just excuses, rationalizations and cop-outs for doing nothing. All can be refuted and none should stop you from letting staff know that what they do is noticed, valued and appreciated. There is no excuse for not doing what should be done.

Temptation #7: Believing Staff Protestations

It is common for recipients to dismiss praise and expressions of appreciation:

"Ah, it was nothing. I was just doing my job."
"Anyone would have done the same thing."
"Really, I didn't do anything. It was the guys on my team."

These protestations should not be interpreted as evidence that the recipients don't want to be recognized. More likely, it shows that because recognition can be so rare, some people are unsure how to respond graciously with a simple, "Thank you."

In workshops, I have asked participants, "Who feels they get too much recognition? You just want to go to your supervisor and say, 'Boss, I just can't take any more of this recognition. Please stop telling me I'm doing a good job. If you can't say something bad to me, don't say anything.' "

I am still waiting for someone to raise her hand and say, "Yeah, that's me! I am always being told that I'm doing a good job. I just can't stand it. All I want to know is when I screw up. There's the one thing I just don't get enough of—negative feedback."

No, I believe that protestations are rooted in the lack of recognition. People just aren't sure how to respond when recognized.

Temptation #8: Becoming Discouraged

There will be setbacks in your efforts to recognize staff.

Some things will not work as well as you feel they should. There will be naysayers. When your efforts fail, analyze what went wrong. Make adjustments and do better next time.

Some people will be cynical about your increased efforts to recognize staff.

"It's the latest fad—the flavour-of-the-month. It won't last."

"He must be reading those management-theory books again."

"I guess she attended a staff recognition workshop at last month's convention and now she's trying it out on us."

"Her boss must have told her that she has to recognize staff more."

If staff has heard only negative feedback in the past, either from you or other supervisors, it will take time for them to believe that times are changing. They will need to see action that backs up your words. You will need to walk the talk.

"Be bold. If you're going to make an error, make a doozy and don't be afraid to hit the ball."
— **Billie Jean King,**
tennis star

Dealing with their suspicions and cynicism will test your patience, but hang in there. What you are doing is what you should be doing, and what nearly every staff member wants.

Focus on what you would like to do better or differently. How could providing recognition make a difference for others and your organization? Set simple, easy-to-achieve goals for yourself. No more than one or two each week. For example:

- To write five thank-you notes per week
- To acknowledge the contributions of at least one staff member every day
- To make recognition more **Timely** by acknowledging staff as soon as I see them performing well
- To learn at least one thing about each of five staff members that could be used to recognize them appropriately

Pause at the end of your work week to assess your progress. How well did you achieve your goals? Should you continue to work toward the same goals next week or create new ones?

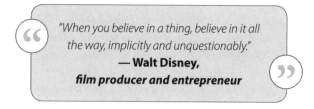

"When you believe in a thing, believe in it all the way, implicitly and unquestionably."
— **Walt Disney,**
film producer and entrepreneur

Making a Commitment to What Matters

Deciding to provide more meaningful recognition begins with a commitment to acknowledging staff. Providing recognition must be something that matters to you. It requires a long-term commitment. Quick fixes don't work. These approaches achieve nothing and will likely make staff more resistant to future staff recognition.

Like other things in life, success with staff recognition requires preparation. You need to develop your skills and assemble tools to make you effective. Check out the recognition toolkit suggestions in Appendix A.

Look at what is happening elsewhere. What are other organizations and supervisors doing? What's working for them? Ask friends and colleagues about their experiences with staff recognition—either as the persons providing the recognition or as recipients. What worked and what didn't?

Reflect on your own experience as a recognition recipient. Remember a time when you were recognized. What makes this experience stand out? What can you learn from this experience—good or bad—that you can apply to your own recognition of staff?

Think also about how you would like to be recognized for performing your job well. Why would this be a good way to recognize you? Would this type of recognition work for your staff?

When it comes to staff recognition, don't just take my word for it. The books listed in Appendix B of this book are all good sources from which to learn more and add to your collection of staff recognition techniques.

Look for opportunities to get training in how to recognize staff. Select sessions on staff recognition when you attend conventions or conferences. If I happen to be presenting, approach me after the session. Identify yourself as someone who has read this book and I will have a gift for you—a tool you can use when recognizing staff.

Consider joining Recognition Professionals International (www.recognition. org) and attending its annual convention, where you will meet and learn from people like you who are committed to staff recognition. RPI conventions attract both people responsible for recognition within their organizations and people who support their efforts with training and recognition tools.

Become the champion of recognition in your workplace. Talk to colleagues about the importance of letting others know they are appreciated. Encourage them to increase the recognition they provide. Share staff recognition techniques that work for you and ask about what they do.

Schedule staff recognition training in your workplace. Most people in supervisory positions weren't put there because of their ability to recognize staff and may be unsure how to do this effectively. Remember that opportunities to express appreciation should not be limited to managers and supervisors. All staff has a role to play and all would benefit from staff recognition training.

Practise Practise Practise

> **Visitor to the Big Apple:** How do I get to Carnegie Hall?
> **New Yorker:** Practise, practise, practise!

It's not enough to learn about how to recognize staff. You need to practise what you learn so you can apply it in your workplace. It's never a good idea to practise on your staff. That would be like a performer who steps on stage without first trying out his new material in a rehearsal hall.

There are better places to practise:

At home – Tell your spouse, kids or friends what you appreciate about what they do. They will welcome your positive messages.

Away from home – When you get good service in a store or a restaurant, let the service provider know how you feel about what she did. It's likely not the type of feedback they normally receive, and it just may ensure that you get good service on your next visit. By the way, even if you praise the person who serves your meal, you should still leave a tip.

In writing – Think about a teacher that made a difference in your life. Write that teacher a letter to let her know how much you appreciated what you learned in her classroom. Be specific about what you learned and describe how you have applied it to your life. Teachers often never see the results of their work, or understand their impact on the lives of former students. Your recognition may not be **Timely,** but if it is **Genuine** it will be truly appreciated.

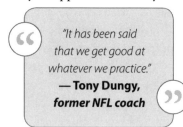

"It has been said that we get good at whatever we practice."
— **Tony Dungy, former NFL coach**

If you can't track down any former teachers, write a note to someone who you heard speak at a conference. Tell him what elements of his presentation you found particularly useful. I have been surprised by the responses when I have done this. Two speakers responded with notes of their own and another even looked me up at the association's conference a year later to express appreciation for my thank-you note.

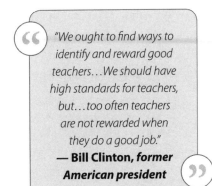

> "We ought to find ways to identify and reward good teachers…We should have high standards for teachers, but…too often teachers are not rewarded when they do a good job."
> — **Bill Clinton**, *former American president*

In your mind – Visualize delivering recognition to someone in your office. Why are you recognizing this person? What are you saying or doing? How does it feel to recognize this person? How is she receiving the recognition? How does she seem to feel about the recognition?

In front of your mirror – Rehearse your recognition delivery. Observe your gestures and facial expression. What you see is what the recipient will see (except maybe for the part about you being in your jammies). Is your body language in sync with what you are saying? Does it help make your message of appreciation seem **Genuine?**

A Morning Reminder

Attach a note to the mirror in your bathroom, where you will see it first thing every day before going to work, to remind you to recognize staff.

During your practice, keep the acronym **GREAT** in mind. Before you say or do anything, you must genuinely believe that what the person did is worthy of recognition. Then strengthen your message by making it **Relevant, Explicit, Appropriate** and **Timely.**

Oh yes, there is one other opportunity to practise:

On the phone – Surprise telemarketers by telling them how much you enjoy getting their calls. Thank them for the valuable information or great deals they have for you.

Okay. I know, I know. This won't be **Genuine** recognition. But there may be another benefit beyond the opportunity to practise your recognition techniques. The telemarketer may be so shocked by your praise that he will voluntarily put you on the do-not-call list.

 "How wonderful it is that nobody need wait a single minute before starting to improve the world."
— **Anne Frank,** *writer*

At Least 20 Ways to Enhance Staff Recognition

1. Put staff recognition on your to-do list—not once, but every day.
2. Recognize people for doing common, everyday tasks well. Don't withhold your recognition until something spectacular happens. After all, who staff are and what they do everyday creates the basis for a spectacular future. If they weren't performing routine tasks correctly, the only spectacular thing the future will hold will be your company's failure.
3. Schedule 15 minutes each day to express appreciation—time to write thank-you notes, to visit staff members' work stations to offer a few words of praise, or to make a phone call to express gratitude.
4. Leave your office with only one objective in mind—to find someone doing his job well. Acknowledge her contribution before returning to your office. Even better, seek out one more staff member whose efforts you can praise before returning to your office.
5. Carry something in your pocket—a special coin, a poker chip, a pebble— that will remind you of the importance of staff recognition every time you touch it.
6. Visit employees' workstations to learn more about what they do and what they need to do their tasks effectively.
7. Focus on just one staff member for an entire day. Observe what he does well. Meet with him before the end of the day. Describe what you saw him do well, and why what he does is important to the success of the organization. Relate your observations to the company's mission statement and goals.
8. Promise yourself a reward when you have successfully recognized each staff member at least once—a massage, a movie night, dinner at your favourite restaurant.

9. Schedule a meeting with each staff member during which you will focus on just one topic—how she contributes to the organization and how what she does fits into the larger picture.

10. Think about what you look for when hiring someone new. Are these the same traits and behaviours for which you are recognizing staff? If not, they should be.

11. What behaviours are necessary to fulfill the mission and goals of your organization? What actions reflect its values? They are the behaviours and actions for which staff should be recognized. Doing so will make recognition **Relevant**.

12. Listen and watch for behaviours that warrant recognition. Acknowledge them when you see them. Praise good work in a **Timely** way and as often as possible.

13. Encourage peer recognition. Invite staff to thank their co-workers for their support and assistance.

14. Assemble a group of trusted advisors. Ask them for advice and feedback. Make them recognition partners.

15. Create a list of words that say, "Good job!" Here are a few to get you started: Terrific! Amazing results! Dazzling work! Outstanding work! Well done! Excellent!

16. Demonstrate the importance of staff recognition by scheduling time at the beginning of staff meetings for you and others to recognize co-workers. Recognition should never be relegated to the end of the meeting—after we have dealt with all the "important" stuff.

17. Anticipate and plan for future recognition opportunities—when a report is due, the expected completion date for a project, or the anniversary of someone joining your team.

18. Select one of your organization's values (teamwork, customer service, innovation) as the staff recognition focus for the week. Watch for examples of behaviours that reflect that value. When you see it, speak to the person. Describe what you saw, explain why it is important and express your appreciation.

19. If you are in a position to influence the process, hire people with a track record as recognizers. (For more on what to ask during interviews to identify people with staff recognition skills, see Chapter 28, "Hire Recognizers and Those Who Have Been Recognized")

20. And train the rest of your staff to recognize, too.

Begin with a Staff List

A list of the staff you supervise can be used in several ways as an aid to your staff recognition efforts:

- Next to each name on your list, write down something this staff member does with which you are pleased. Have you told her this is something you appreciate? Have you told her recently? Is it time to tell her again?
- At the beginning of the week, commit to recognizing each person on your list at least once before the week ends. Use the list to keep score.
- What do you know about each employee as a person? What are his non-work interests and hobbies? What is his favourite treat? Is he married? What is his spouse's name? Do they have children? Once you have this and other information, how can you use what you know to provide **Appropriate** recognition?
- Create a second list of recognition techniques you would like to use. Match the employees' names to the techniques. Which technique(s) would be most **Appropriate** for each individual?

"The best time to plant a tree is twenty years ago.
The second best time is now."
— Chinese Proverb

DIY RECOGNITION RESEARCH:
The 10-Day Recognition Challenge

What you will need for this research project:
Someone whose relationship is important to you—a family member, friend or co-worker; two minutes a day for 10 consecutive days

Research Plan:
Once a day, for 10 days, share with this person a different quality or trait that you admire, appreciate or value about him.

Guidelines:
- If you start the process, be committed to finishing it.
- Select someone you with whom you are in contact daily.
- Choose a partner with whom you have a healthy relationship.
- Tell the person what you are doing.

> *"I am working on doing a better job of letting people who are important to me know how much I appreciate their contribution to our workplace (or our family, community, this friendship, etc.). Since you are one of those persons for me, would it be all right if once a day over the next 10 days, I share a different quality, attribute, or trait that I admire and appreciate about you?"*

- Share the traits in person.
- Give a specific example for each trait or quality that is shared.
- Set an agreed upon time and place when and where you will share the traits.
- Ask your partner to accept your comment gracefully. A simple "Thank you" is sufficient.
- Be open to discovering traits and qualities along the way.
- Keep a list of traits as you go along.
- One trait a day—no accumulation or "catching up."
- Thank the person at the end. Give the person your list.

Inspired by *Thirty Days to a Happy Employee: How a Simple Program of Acknowledgment Can Build Trust and Loyalty at Work* by Dottie Bruce Gandy (Toronto: Simon & Schuster, 2001, ISBN 068487329X).

Implications for the Workplace:
- How difficult was it to come up with traits to appreciate?
- How did it feel the first time you expressed appreciation? How did this change over the 10 days?
- How did the other person respond the first few times you identified a trait? How did this change over the 10 days?

Hint: Once you begin to look for reasons to recognize people you begin to find them. Once you begin to recognize people, they begin to anticipate and look forward to being recognized.

Chapter 26
Finding Behaviour to Celebrate

There is a simple answer to the question, "What should I recognize?"

Recognize any behaviours you would like to see more of!

Meaningful recognition should be triggered when desired behaviours are observed, not by dates on the calendar.

- Praise contributions that help your organization achieve its goals.
- Acknowledge actions that are consistent with your organization's values.
- Express appreciation for behaviours that relate to what the individual or team needs to do to be successful.
- Recognize those who help create the type of work environment that you wish to see.

"The things that get rewarded get done. If you aren't getting the results you want, ask the magic question: 'What's being rewarded?'"
— Michael LeBoeuf, *GMP: The Greatest Management Principle in the World*

On the other hand, you should:

- Avoid unintentionally rewarding the wrong behaviours.
- Ignore behaviours that are not relevant to individual, team or organizational success, unless they are potentially damaging, such as behaviours that:

  – Tarnish the organization's reputation
  – Endanger the safety of employees or customers
  – Reduce productivity
  – Undermine staff morale
  – Increase costs
  – Are illegal or unethical

When looking for opportunities to recognize staff, remember that it is not just about outcomes. Consider sports teams and their fans. While they celebrate outcomes—victories and championships—they also celebrate every success along the way—every goal, every touchdown, every hit. Why should things be different for work teams?

Acknowledging progress keeps people focused and engaged in the larger task. Describe what has gone well so far, and express confidence that goals will be met and projects will be completed successfully.

Recognition is about the many small things that are done well every day, not just about a few big things done extraordinarily well—although these are certainly important and should be acknowledged when they occur.

People do things every day that are worthy of praise—small things that when done well contribute to the organization's success. Small actions can make the job easier for others and contribute to the quality of workplace life.

To be able to observe and praise small, but important contributions, supervisors need to know staff members well enough to know what they do well. Then they need to find ways for them to use these skills, which will create opportunities for staff to be recognized for the way they contribute.

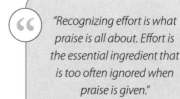

> "Recognizing effort is what praise is all about. Effort is the essential ingredient that is too often ignored when praise is given."
> — **Sharon F. Marks,**
> ***It Pays to Praise***

When recognition is only focused on those big, easy-to-see contributions and achievements—"going above and beyond the call of duty"—it can be discouraging to many staff members. They feel that they will never meet such a high standard.

Of course, the standard itself can be confusing. What to one supervisor is "above and beyond" is just a normal performance to another.

When only the top performers are praised, it means most staff members miss out on what they most want most from their jobs—to be appreciated for what they do. Praise is powerful as a means of motivating people to do what you want to them doing more. Praise is much more powerful than the alternatives—criticism, reprimands or punishment.

"Take a minute. Look at your goals. Look at your performance. See if your behavior matches your goals."
— Ken Blanchard & Spenser Johnson,
The One Minute Manager

Visit www.GREATstaffrecognition.com/bookbonus/behaviours for examples of behaviours that reflect a few of the values that organizations commonly set for themselves.

DIY RECOGNITION RESEARCH:
First Steps or First Marathon

What you will need for this research project:
A toddler, a least one parent (if you can't find a parent, a grandparent will do)

Research Process:
Observe what happens when the toddler takes his first steps. How do the parents (or grandparents) react?

- ❏ With excitement, cheering every step the child takes. There are lots of hugs and the child is always picked up when he falls and encouraged to try again.

- ❏ Without emotion. After all, it's no big deal. All children learn to walk. "We'll cheer when he completes his first marathon."

Implications for the workplace:
What are you recognizing? Outcomes, final products and completed projects or day-to-day progress and contributions?

Hint: It is important to recognize both.

Chapter 27
Doing Recognition Right

Emotions evoke particularly strong memories. You are more likely to remember how you felt than what happened, what was said, or what you received on the day…

- You graduated from high school, college or university
- You were married
- You began your first real job or received your first promotion
- Your team won the championship (unless you are a Toronto Maple Leafs fan, in which case you are likely not old enough—or too old—to remember the last time the team won the Stanley Cup)

Being recognized for doing a good job can be like that, too. What is said and how it is said is more important that any gift presented to mark an employee's contributions or achievements. The quality of the presentation determines the value of the recognition in the mind of the recipient. Presentations that are well made validate the person and what he did. People remember how something was presented and how that made them feel, better than they remember what they received.

Unless You Are the Queen

During a stay at Ashford Castle, County Mayo, Ireland, I discovered a letter, framed and displayed on a wall. It read:

> *Rick Lewis,*
> *Ashford Castle resident artist*
>
> *The Queen has commanded me to thank you for your letter of 20 May, which she read with much interest, and the enclosed photographs.*
>
> *Kenneth Scott*

If you are a monarch, it may be acceptable to "command" your private secretary to express appreciation on your behalf. But for the rest of us, recognition is not something to delegate. It just wouldn't seem **Genuine.** People on your staff who deserve to be recognized deserve to be recognized by you.

If the recognition was delivered by the right person, at the right time, in the right place and in the right way, the emotional memory will be positive. If the person, time, place or manner of recognition was wrong, the memory may be less pleasant. If all or most of these ingredients were wrong, the emotions associated with this event may be negative, or at best neutral.

There is an exception to the generalization that the gift or award is less important than how it's presented. That is when the item is disproportional to the achievement or contribution being acknowledged. When this happens, it can be confusing or hurtful for the recipient.

> *"The manner of giving is worth more than the gift."*
> — **Pierre Corneille,**
> *Le Menteur*

Presenting a paper certificate to thank the person who identified how to cut costs by millions of dollars does not reflect the value of the accomplishment. On the other hand, a expensive gift such as a big-screen TV or a vacation trip would be inappropriate for someone who did a good job of cleaning up the staff break room.

Once again, the emotional memory of the recognition will likely outlive what was received—but for the wrong reasons.

Ensuring that the recognition you deliver is at the right time, in the right place and in the right way–we will assume you are the right person–is a matter of planning, whether the recognition is formal or informal.

At first glance, this may appear to contradict what I have written elsewhere. Informal day-to-day recognition–especially when it is **Timely**–is often spontaneous. But this does not mean that how the recognition is delivered should not be thought out ahead of time. "Winging it" is unlikely to produce a meaningful recognition experience for the recipient.

> " *"It appears that the techniques that have the greatest motivational impact are practiced the least even though they are easier and less expensive to use."*
> **—Dr. Gerald Graham, Wichita State University** "

"Planning" means being prepared to recognize whenever the opportunities arise. It enables you to provide recognition that is **Relevant, Explicit** and **Appropriate.** Planning means doing your research ahead of time, getting to know staff members and what manner of recognition would be **Appropriate.** This knowledge comes from conversations with the employee, her co-workers, family and friends.

Planning also means knowing what's important—the organization's values and goals and what behaviours are critical to its success. Knowing this prepares you to choose your words properly and create connections between what you observed and are praising, and what is important.

Recognizing people in the right way may involve inviting others—co-workers, family, even the company's mascot—to join the celebration. Some organizations have a special signal—a bell, a tune played over the intercom, a blast on a horn—that calls staff to gather for the celebration of a colleague's success.

Recognition in 3-D

Describe what happened
Discuss the impact
Do something to show appreciation
— Source unknown

Staff Recognition Dos and Don'ts

Do

- Add staff recognition to your daily to-do list.
- Describe what the individual or team did and why it is important.
- Invite others who know the recipient and what she did to join the celebration or add their comments.
- Keep track of who you recognize and why. Also note who you are missing. Is there something for which you could recognize them?
- Link the performance being recognized to the organization's goals and values. Recognition brings these concepts to life.

Don't

- Be unprepared. Know who you are recognizing, including his name, and understand how he contributed.
- Embarrass the recipient, especially someone who is shy. Embarrassment is a strong, negative emotion.
- Promise what you can't deliver (e.g. "John will have a position with us for many years to come.")
- Leave a certificate, plaque or gift on her desk without any explanation, or tell them to pick it up from the HR department.
- Save up recognition for some future "special moment," recognition event or performance appraisal.

The right way to recognize may be to praise in public or one-on-one in the privacy of an office. You could visit her office or workspace, or invite the recipient to your office.

Sometimes praise will be delivered only once, other times the recognition can be repeated. A commendation delivered in private can be repeated in public. Praise that's spoken first can later be provided to the recipient in writing. Actions for which a person is recognized today could also be referenced on her annual performance appraisal in the future. The impact of recognition increases when it's repeated.

Variety is the Spice of Recognition

Recognizing the right way may mean recognizing in different ways at different times. Varying how you recognize people adds excitement. The element of the unexpected makes recognition special and memorable.

Sometimes recognition is delivered in person and sometimes in writing. Sometimes recognition occurs in private; other times in public. There may be a small gift on one occasion, a favourite treat on another.

Whenever you deliver recognition in person, keep these guidelines in mind:

- Keep it short and simple. A minute or less is often enough time. Say what the person did, why it was important and that it is appreciated. Then, move on. Expressions of gratitude that go on and on begin to sound insincere. The supervisor appears unsure about what is being recognized, and why. Maybe she believes that if she rambles on long enough, something will eventually resonate with the recipient.

"Simplicity is the ultimate sophistication."
— Leonardo da Vinci

- Establish and maintain eye contact with the recipient. This creates a feeling of comfort and conveys a message of sincerity.
- Know and use the recipient's first name. Pronounce it correctly and avoid nicknames that the recipient doesn't normally use.
- Remember that recognition delivered in private seems more **Genuine.** There is no audience to impress—no reason to suspect the supervisor's motives. Private recognition builds trust that is necessary for public recognition to be effective.
- Smile. This is a happy occasion. A time to celebrate. Let your body language show it.

SAIL Into Recognition

Use this formula to tell the story of staff members' achievements or contributions:

> **Situation** – that the staff member helped with
> **Action** – that he took
> **Impact** – that his action had on the organization
> **Link** – it all back to the organization's values and goals

Adapted from *The Daily Carrot Principle: 365 Ways to Enhance Your Career and Life* by Adrian Gostick and Chester Elton (Toronto: Free Press, 2010 ISBN 9781439181737)

More Powerful than a Sword...or Email

Every year, post office statistics show a decline in the number of first class letters delivered. In part this may be because more of us are paying bills and doing other business online.

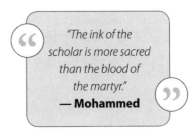

> *"The ink of the scholar is more sacred than the blood of the martyr."*
> — **Mohammed**

But it is also because fewer of us are writing letters. When you think about it, can you remember the last time you found a personal, handwritten letter in your mailbox? For many, it has been years.

Putting our expressions of appreciation in writing does not mean writing formal letters, on company letterhead, as some managers feel is necessary to validate the recognition they provide. (They also feel a copy needs to be placed in the employee's personnel file, which seems to demonstrate that the manager does recognize staff, more than to provide any benefit to the recipient.)

While there is nothing wrong with letters that come from a computer printer, the nature of written recognition can be much simpler—on a sheet of paper left on a desk, a sticky note attached to a document or a computer screen, or a handwritten thank-you note.

Because they are so rare, the impact of handwritten messages of appreciation are powerful—and memorable. The handwritten message conveys a sense of the recognition being **Genuine.** The writer made the extra effort to write it by hand. It is unique. The writer's gesture stands out in a world dominated by technology. It's always a good time to express appreciation with a handwritten thank-you card.

Often recipients will save these notes of appreciation, pinning them to their office walls or keeping them in their desks. Rereading them later can be reassuring, especially on those days when things are not going well. People don't treat emails the same way. Emails are seldom saved. Most are deleted soon after being read, and sometimes, without being read.

> *"The handwritten thank you is a modest engagement. It probably won't save lives, but it just might boost your odds of becoming rich, famous and adored. (Not to mention making you feel a lot better about yourself.)"*
> — **Tom Peters, *business guru***

Supervisors should always carry a supply of thank-you cards with them. Having cards with you prepares you to take a few minutes at any time to express gratitude—while waiting for an appointment, on an airplane, or in a coffee shop. Writing a few thank-you notes is a good way to de-stress at the end of the day. Is there a better way to recover from a hectic day than with positive thoughts associated with thanking staff members for their contributions?

My preference is to use green ink when writing thank-you notes. Blue or purple ink also works, but I always avoid using black or red. A card written with a black pen looks like it could have come from a photocopier. As for red…well, we all remember what red ink meant during our school days!

Green is well-suited to staff recognition. It is a calm, refreshing colour that is commonly associated with life, nature and growth. For drivers everywhere, green means 'Go.' In Europe, green exit signs show the way to safety. The word green is closely related to the Old English verb grenian, which means "to grow." In ancient Greece, green symbolized victory. Green is associated with the peaceful Irish countryside (and beer on St. Patrick's Day), and in Scotland it is a mark of honour. Islam venerates green, as it expects paradise to be full of lush greenery.

One Minute Praising

1. Let people know that you will provide feedback on their performance.
2. Praise immediately after you see deserving behaviour.
3. Be specific about what the person did right.
4. Describe how good you feel about what the person did and how it helps the company and other people who work there.
5. Stop talking for a moment to allow the person to feel how good you feel.
6. Encourage more of the same behaviour.
7. Shake hands or tap the person on the shoulder to show your support of their success.

Adapted from *The One Minute Manager* by Ken Blanchard and Spencer Johnson (New York: Berkley Books, 1984) ISBN 0688014291

Here are a few tips for writing **GREAT** thank-you notes:

- Write your note as soon as possible after the event or action that prompted you to thank an individual or team (**Timely**)
- Be specific when describing what the person did that you appreciate (**Explicit**)
- Describe the impact on the company of the employee's action—refer to values, goals or mission statement—and/or the impact on the person expressing gratitude (**Relevant**)

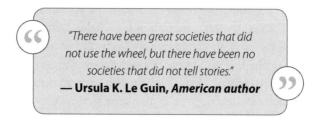

> "There have been great societies that did not use the wheel, but there have been no societies that did not tell stories."
> — **Ursula K. Le Guin, *American author***

Telling Stories of Success

Storytelling is a powerful staff recognition tool. Stories create emotional connections between people and events for which recognition is given. Listeners feel they were there. Stories can lead to morals that allow the teller to reinforce the organization's values and goals.

"Yesterday, as I was walking through the front office, I noticed Ed dealing with a customer who appeared upset. I stopped to watch what was going on, prepared to offer my assistance if it was needed. It wasn't. Ed did a masterful job of diffusing the situation. He listened to what the customer was saying, then asked two or three questions to clarify her concerns.

"Apparently she was unhappy about something she had bought here a few days earlier. It wasn't working the way she thought it should. Ed said he hadn't received any other complaints about this product, but maybe there was something wrong with the one she had bought. He offered to test it himself. When he couldn't make it work either, he gave the customer the option of exchanging the defective one for a new one or getting her money back. When she requested a

replacement, he got a new one from stock. He offered to take the new one out of its packaging and check to make sure it operated properly. This gave him the opportunity to go through the operating instructions with the client. After checking it out, Ed returned it to the package and the woman left with her product, obviously much happier than when she had come in.

"We all know that one of our values is quality customer service and we have a goal to improve our customer retention by five per cent this year. Ed took advantage of this opportunity to provide great service that may ensure that this customer will continue to do business with us. When we do whatever is necessary to provide quality service to each of our customers, our action reflects the value we put on customer service and helps us meet our customer-retention goal."

Fun and Funny...

Whatever business you are in—whether it's education, health care, government, manufacturing, retail or mining—should be taken seriously. But that doesn't mean that work can't be fun and the workplace filled with humour.

Having fun at work is important. Having fun reduces work-related stress and creates workplaces where people want to be. In *301 Ways to Have Fun at Work,* Dave Hemsath and Leslie Yerkes express their belief that "fun at work may be the single most important trait of a highly effective and successful organization; we see a direct link between fun at work and employee creativity, productivity, morale, satisfaction, and retention, as well as customer service and many other factors that determine business success."

Employees appreciate supervisors who have a sense of humour. In the November 8, 2007 issue, *USA Today* reported that 97 per cent of respondents to a Robert Half International survey answered yes when asked, "Is it important for managers to have a sense of humour?"

Like other aspects of your business, the need to recognize staff should be taken seriously, but doesn't mean that staff recognition always has to be serious and formal. It can be fun and include humour.

Using humour when recognizing staff is a great way to grab people's attention and make the recognition memorable. Humour can make recognition fun, while also conveying a strong message of appreciation:

- Gardening gloves for someone who "lends a helping hand."
- A package of microwave popcorn for "popping into action."
- A toy giraffe for an employee who was prepared to "stick his neck out" (take a risk).
- A plant when a staff member's contributions "helped the organization grow."
- A puzzle for someone who has become "an important piece of our organization."
- Tickets to a sporting event or concert for "being a ticket to our success."
- A calculator for the newcomer who is "a great addition to our staff."
- A highlighter for when working with someone "was a career highlight."

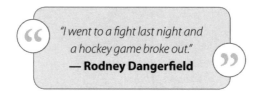

> *"I went to a fight last night and a hockey game broke out."*
> — **Rodney Dangerfield**

…But It's No Joking Matter

While the presentation or gift may be humourous, it should always come with a positive message that includes an **Explicit** description of the performance or achievement for which the recipient is being recognized. Neither the person or his accomplishment should treated as a joke.

There are stand-up comedy wannabes who turn recognition occasions into roasts. Their attempts to add humour can turn celebrations into negative experiences. To generate laughs, the person who should be acknowledging contributions focuses on some aspect of the recipient's appearance or behaviour.

> *"Maybe we should have given George a gift certificate for a new tie. Where did you get that one…at clown school?"*

> *"Shirley, you did a great job of incorporating current research into this report, which I'm sure surprised everyone, given the condition of your desk. I'm surprised you can find anything in that mess!"*

Some supervisors feel that the most effective way to change behaviour is through ridicule and public embarrassment. They present negative "awards," such as "slow poke" awards to those who regularly show up late for meetings, a special name badge for failing to meet performance goals, or a giant eraser to correct foolish mistakes.

Embarrassment is a powerful emotion, which is more likely to demoralize than motivate change. Recipients begin looking for the nearest exit. Co-workers feel badly for the ridiculed individual and resentment towards the person who delivered the negative award.

Such perverted use of staff recognition is symptomatic of supervisory cowardice. Where they exist, performance problems should be addressed directly, through coaching, training or disciplinary action. Never with public humiliation.

Excuses, Rationalizations and Cop-outs (Part IV)

"No one else around here is doing it. I don't want to be the only one."

Imagine a company where recognition begins at the top. Everyone, at every level, is encouraged to recognize staff. And they are good at it. The CEO is generous in her use of praise when dealing with staff. This spirit of appreciation cascades through the different levels of management to those on the front line. With their superiors as role models, supervisors skillfully and consistently recognize their staff.

What an ideal place to work. But it doesn't sound like the place where you work. You can't remember the last time your boss said anything positive about your work. In this environment, it's hard to be motivated to recognize your staff. Stop waiting for the top guy to initiate meaningful staff recognition practices. It's up to you.

For your staff, it's not about your boss. Whether he does a good job of recognizing staff, or not, doesn't matter. It is about you. Your staff isn't waiting in anxious anticipation to hear words of appreciation from the CEO, or some other seldom-seen executive. The recognition they most want–and the recognition that will be most meaningful–is the recognition that will come from you.

Stop waiting for the recognition ball to roll down the organization. Take action. You can get things started. Say thank you to those who you supervise. Say thank you to your co-workers. Find reasons to express appreciation to your boss for what your boss does. The recognition bug might just be catching.

The companies whose names appear in various lists of "Best Places to Work" are not there because they pay better than others or offer outstanding benefits, although they may do both. What stands out is what they do to create a place where people want to be. They treat staff well, including recognizing them for performing their jobs well. Potential employees, especially younger ones, are attracted to organizations that have reputations for treating staff well.

 "You must be the change you want to see in the world."
— **Mahatma Gandhi, *Indian political leader***

"We tried recognizing people once—it didn't work.
We won't make that mistake twice."

Sometimes executives feel that what is needed is a big event to show staff they are appreciated—a formal dinner or a company picnic. And of course, there should be hundreds of certificates or plaques and gifts emblazoned with the company logo.

Then the corporate leadership sits back and waits for engagement to increase, motivation to improve and productivity to soar. When nothing changes, the executives are surprised and hurt. "They said they wanted more recognition, so we gave it to them. But they don't seem to appreciate what we did for them."

Initial recognition efforts may fail because they are incongruent with the prevailing culture. There is little recognition that precedes the event and nothing happens afterwards. Expressing and receiving appreciation will be foreign to a culture where it has not been the practice. It seems to appear out of the blue. Staff may be skeptical about the motives of those who are recognizing them. The approach used to recognize staff may not be **Appropriate** for the employees or the workplace.

Introducing new practices into a workplace can be difficult. Few techniques work as the well the first time we use them as we hope they will. Innovation takes time. There are few overnight success stories. Workplace cultures don't change quickly. It requires persistence. You have to stick with it.

> *"Success seems to be largely a matter of*
> *hanging on after others have let go."*
> **— William Feather, *American publisher and author***

"I might miss someone. After all, I can't be everywhere at once. I can't
always see what each employee does or achieves."

Better to miss someone's contributions some of the time, than to be seen as ignoring everyone's contributions and achievements all the time. People are likely to forgive the occasional oversight as long as they don't feel that what they do is never seen or valued. If you regularly recognize others for what they do, staff will understand about the occasional omission. After all, no one–not even teachers–have eyes in the back of their heads.

To ensure that no individual is consistently missed, keep track of who is being recognized, when and for what. Enlist others in your plans to increase the amount of recognition staff receives. Encourage staff to recognize co-workers. Peer recognition increases the frequency with which people are acknowledged, exponentially.

"It's not my job."

If not you, then who? The people in the human resources department? The CEO?

Ask staff about these people, and they'll tell you that they never see them. Who do they see every day? Their supervisor. This person's opinion matters. Staff members want their direct supervisor to know what they do and to care about them. When supervisors express appreciation, they show that they know and care.

Sometimes, supervisors believe that their job is just about productivity; getting the work done. What is more productive than a motivated and engaged workforce? The way to increase its motivation and engagement is with a regular dose of recognition.

"Do not wait for leaders; do it alone, person to person."
— **Mother Teresa,** *religious leader*

"Knowing that they have done a good job should be reward enough."

For some, it is. These are people who have reached the pinnacle of Abraham Maslow's hierarchy of needs: self-actualization.

However, many have not reached this point. Maslow described their needs as social and self-esteem. People need to have their value and self-worth affirmed by others–including and in many cases, most importantly–by the person who oversees their work on a daily basis.

Today's affirmation may be the spark that ignites their future self-actualization.

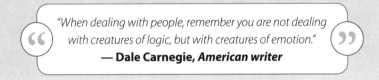

"When dealing with people, remember you are not dealing with creatures of logic, but with creatures of emotion."
— **Dale Carnegie,** *American writer*

Chapter 28
Hire Recognizers and Those Who Have Been Recognized

Hiring decisions should always be based on performance-related factors. Does the candidate have the training, skills and experience required to perform successfully? Has he done the *right* things the *right* way in previous work situations?

If recognition is important to your organization, the ability to acknowledge the contributions of others effectively is something you should look for when filling vacant positions—especially supervisory positions. Include at least one question about staff recognition when interviewing candidates.

How you ask about staff recognition—and about any other competency or expectation for that matter—will make a big difference to the quality of information you receive in the candidate's response. When an interviewer asks, "What are your thoughts about staff recognition?" or "Why do you feel supervisors should recognize staff for doing good work?" the candidate is likely to respond with an explanation of the importance of staff recognition. Ask, "How would you recognize a staff member for doing a good job?" and the response will likely include what he thinks he *would* do or what he thinks *you* would want him to do.

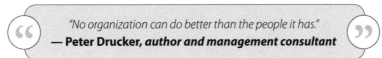

"No organization can do better than the people it has."
— **Peter Drucker, *author and management consultant***

The candidate's answer may sound good, but it is just theory. This is not enough. You need more. You need evidence that the candidate has recognized staff in the past and has done it well. While people can always be trained to recognize others (after all, that is what I train people to do), the ideal situation is to hire people with a track record as recognizers.

You want people who have recognized others for their contributions or achievement effectively, appropriately and frequently. Based on what you hear, you can predict how effectively the candidate will recognize others if you offer him a position. Here is a question that will uncover evidence of whether the candidate in front of you has or has not recognized others effectively:

> *Describe a time when you recognized someone you supervised or a co-worker for doing his or her job well.*

I know. It's not exactly a question. But it should get the candidate talking and providing the facts you are looking for. If necessary, be prepared to use these supplementary questions to prompt the candidate to provide more information:

Behaviour Description Interviewing

This question is written in a behaviour description interview style, which is based on the premise that past performance is the best predictor of future performance. For this reason, it is important to require the candidate to answer questions only in the past tense. Don't accept answers that include reference to what she "will do." To learn more about BDI and other aspects of recruiting and selecting staff, visit www.seaconsultingonline.com/Articles/Recruitment/index.htm.

When did this happen?

You are interested if the candidate offers a recent example, preferably one that occurred within the last few days or weeks.

You are not interested if the candidate doesn't offer a recent example. (If necessary, say, *"Please give us a more recent example."*)

What did this person do that you felt deserved to be recognized?

You are interested if the candidate supplies an **Explicit** description of the behaviour for which the other person was recognized.

You are not interested if the candidate generalizes, such as saying, "for doing a good job," or, "he is always helping others," or, "she has worked for us for five years." (If necessary, say, *"Give us a specific example of a way he helped others."*)

How was what this person did important to the success of XYZ Corporation?

You are interested if the behaviour being described is **Relevant** to the corporation's goals, mission and values, or what is important to on-the-job success.

You are not interested if the candidate fails to refer to the corporation's goals and values, or on-the-job success.

When did you find about what the person had done? How soon after that were you able to tell him (her) that he (she) had done a good job?

You are interested if the recognition occurred within a few days or a couple of weeks of the behaviour being observed. The closer the recognition followed the event, the more interested you should be.

You are not interested if the recognition did not occur within two weeks of the candidate learning about the other's contribution or achievement, or the candidate's only act of recognition was to nominate the individual for an award that would be presented months later.

Prior to this time, when was the last time you had recognized this person?

You are interested if there is evidence of the candidate providing recognition frequently.

You are not interested if it was more than a month. You are definitely not interested if the answer is, "Never."

How did you determine how best to recognize this person?

You are interested if the candidate personalized the recognition for each individual.

You are not interested if the candidate recognized everyone in the same way or always relied on the corporation's recognition program.

What did you say when recognizing this person?

You are interested if the candidate said or wrote something specific about what the person did.

You are not interested if the candidate's comments consisted of a general acknowledgement of the individual.

You may not always be successful in finding someone who has a history of recognizing staff effectively, and will hire someone based on other strengths the candidate possesses. Under these circumstances, you must make your expectations related to staff recognition clear to your new hire. Include information about staff recognition as part of the newcomer's orientation. Provide opportunities for the new person to be trained to recognize staff effectively.

Keeping Expectations Alive

The expectations you have when hiring must also be part of the workplace culture. A senior manager who attended one of my recognition workshops seemed to get this. On his evaluation at the end of the day, he wrote that he intended to add staff recognition to the agenda of his weekly meetings with supervisors. "How have you recognized staff during the past week?"

Be Prepared to Recognize New Hires Appropriately

An interview can be a time to learn about a job candidate's experience as a person being recognized. Has she been recognized previously? How does she respond to recognition?

It is also a time to learn about the candidate's recognition preferences. The purpose of asking recognition-related questions is not to hire people whose recognition preferences match your recognition practices. Rather, think of it as early reconnaissance that will be useful if the candidate is hired. Answers to these questions can provide insight into how best to use recognition to motivate a new staff member and sow the seeds of retention. During the interview, you might ask:

- How do you like to be recognized when you have done a good job?
- Describe a time when you were recognized for doing a task well. What made that recognition most memorable?
- Tell us about a time when you did something for which you deserved to be recognized, but weren't. How did this make you feel? What type of recognition would have been **Appropriate** under these circumstances?

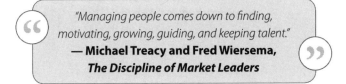

"Managing people comes down to finding, motivating, growing, guiding, and keeping talent."
— **Michael Treacy and Fred Wiersema,**
The Discipline of Market Leaders

Ask Departing Staff, 'How Could We Improve Recognition?'

Information obtained through exit interviews can be used to assess your staff recognition efforts and make adjustments to improve staff morale, engagement and retention.

Typically, exit interviews consist of a few quick questions, asked after an employee has resigned, but before he leaves. They often appear to be done more to fulfill a requirement than motivated by a true desire to learn from what the departing employee has to say. As a result, the person conducting the interview learns little.

Here are two suggestions to increase the value of exit interviews:

- Have someone other than the departing employee's supervisor conduct the interview—a supervisor from another department, a human resources professional, or a neutral third party such as an outside consultant.
- Conduct the exit interview after, rather than before the employee leaves. People who still have a few days left may be reluctant to express their true feelings for fear of offending someone, or of damaging their relationship with their supervisor or co-workers. People who have left and settled in their new jobs may feel less constrained.

"Equipment and real estate may be bought and sold, but the company with excellent employees enjoys the most priceless, hard-to-find, and sought-after asset."
— **Jan Carlzon, *former CEO, Scandinavian Airlines***

DIY RECOGNITION RESEARCH:
But You Could Do Better

What you will need for this research project:
30 minutes during a staff meeting

Procedure:
1. Have staff members divide themselves into pairs.

2. Ask each person to think of a reason to compliment his partner (clothing, how he handles a work-related task, his sense of humour) and a way in which this aspect of his life could be improved.

3. Have the partners take turns offering feedback, beginning with what he likes about his partner, followed by "but" and a description of what could be better, e.g. "I like the way you arranged the furniture in your office, but you should have a place for visitors to put their coffee cups."

4. Ask, "How did it feel to receive a compliment, followed by the word 'but'?" "What does it usually mean when a person says something positive, followed by a 'but'?"

Implications for the Workplace:
How often does but—or similar words such as however, nevertheless, although or on the other hand—signal to the listener that she should disregard what she just heard? The important message follows the but.

Hint: The word "but" is a verbal eraser. It makes everything that went before it irrelevant.

Chapter 29
Do You Know What Your Staff Thinks?

A well-known American tycoon is said to have made a practice of taking people he was thinking of hiring for lunch. For our purposes, we will say it was Henry Ford, although others suggest it was J.C. Penny, Thomas Edison, General Douglas MacArthur, Admiral Hyman Rickover or even Howard Hughes.

When the food arrived, Ford would observe the job candidate. If the first thing his guest did–without first tasting his meal–was to add salt or pepper, Ford immediately rejected him as a future employee.

Why? Because Ford was looking for people who would maintain an open mind when encountering new situations. He wanted employees who would seek out the facts, rather than apply solutions based on assumptions.

Is this tale true? Maybe. Maybe not. But does that matter? True or false, this story contains an important lesson that should guide us when making decisions about staff recognition. Base what you do on good information. Know first what is working, what is missing, and what changes are needed.

"The only man who behaves sensibly is my tailor. He takes my measure anew every time he sees me, whilst all the rest go on with their old measurements, and expect them to fit me."
— George Bernard Shaw, *playwright*

You should begin by understanding how your staff feels about recognition. Do they feel appreciated for what they do? Are they told often enough they are doing a good job? Are they being recognized in ways they prefer to be recognized? For the right reasons? By the right people? Have your efforts to recognize staff made a difference?

Without answers to these questions, what you are doing to recognize staff may be a waste of your time and resources. While there are several ways to measure the effectiveness of your staff recognition efforts, such as watching for signs of good or poor morale, examining turnover rates and monitoring productivity levels, the best and simplest way is to ask.

If yours is a small staff (no more than 10 to 15 people), this can be done through face-to-face meetings with small groups or the full staff. Better yet, meet with each staff member individually, beginning with those you predict are most likely to provide honest feedback.

The larger the staff, the less practical it becomes to gather information through individual meetings. Under these circumstances, a survey is a reasonable alternative for collecting staff perceptions about recognition. The time required to draft, administer and interpret the results will be less than would be needed to meet with individual staff members.

When staff can respond to questions anonymously, they may be more candid than when discussing a topic in person. In meetings staff members tend to hold back, fearing that something they could say might offend their supervisor or co-workers. Behind the cloak of anonymity afforded by a survey these same people may feel less constrained.

Dealing with Others' Reality

Before asking–whether face-to-face or by way of a survey–prepare yourself for what you may hear. Approach the listening process with an open mind. Some of what you hear may not be what you want to hear or may make you

> *"Honest criticism is hard to take, particularly from a relative, a friend, an acquaintance, or a stranger."*
> — **Franklin P. Jones, *British engineer and publisher***

feel uncomfortable. Sometimes, our tendency is to dismiss or rationalize feedback that might be perceived as negative, or to denounce those who provide such input.

Resist these temptations. Believe in the feedback you receive. It will accurately reflect how others feel. The perceptions of respondents will be true for

At Least 15 Survey Errors to Avoid

1. The survey is conducted without an intent, and a plan to take action based on the results.
2. The group that is being surveyed is too small. There should be at least 15 people in your sample.
3. The survey is too long. A survey should only take a few minutes.
4. The questions contain jargon and unfamiliar terms. Questions should be direct and use simple language. Avoid jargon if possible and include definitions if its use is necessary.
5. The survey instructions are long and complicated. Instructions should be brief and easy to understand.
6. Timing is bad. Surveys should not be administered at times of crisis or stress, such as just after layoffs are announced or during particularly acrimonious collective bargaining.
7. The most important questions are at the end of the survey. By the time they reach these questions, some respondents may be tired and hurried and will skip these questions altogether.
8. The anonymity and confidentiality of respondents is not respected.
9. The survey asks too many questions. This makes the survey's originator look out-of-touch with what is happening.
10. A survey with too many open-ended questions may look like too much work to complete.
11. Too many topics are explored in one omnibus survey.
12. Questions are actually asking two questions at once: "Do you prefer to be recognized in public, and to be recognized by the CEO or your supervisor?"
13. Questions reflect a bias or have built-in rationalization: "Considering how busy he/she is, do you feel that your supervisor does a good job of recognizing you for your work?"
14. Questions are not grouped logically by topic or type of response requested.
15. There is a long time between when the survey was completed and when the results are available. Circumstances may have changes and people may have lost interest.

those who have them. To deal with the feedback and motivate you and others to act on what is heard, you may want to rephrase negative feedback in more positive language.

Also, commit to work with the information you receive. By asking, you have set expectations that some action will be taken based on what people said. Staff will expect to see positive changes. Fail to act on the information you receive and you will be perceived more negatively than if you had

"Listening can make the difference between a mediocre company and a great one."
— Lee Iacocca

not requested feedback in the first place. If they perceive that nothing has changed as result of their input, the next time staff is asked fewer will respond. Those who do will tend to offer more negative feedback.

Why Conduct a Survey

Before conducting a survey it is important to understand why you are doing so. What do you want to know? And once you know, how will you use this information?

Surveys can serve three purposes:

1. To assess how your staff feels about recognition generally and the recognition they are receiving specifically:
   • Do they feel recognition is important?
   • Do they feel valued for who they are and appreciated for what they do?
   • Do they feel they are being recognized often enough?

2. To learn the best way to recognize staff:
   • How would they like to be recognized?
   • By whom?
   • For what?
   • How often?

3. To establish a benchmark to measure the impact of your recognition efforts over time:
   • Are your staff recognition efforts making any difference?
   • Are satisfaction levels related to recognition improving?

The next step is to decide what questions you will ask. You don't need to, and likely shouldn't, do this on your own. Talk to others. What do other managers and supervisors feel they need to know to assess their effectiveness at recognizing staff and to do a better job? You can also look at what managers and supervisors in other organizations have asked on similar surveys. Can some of their questions be adopted for your survey or adapted for your use?

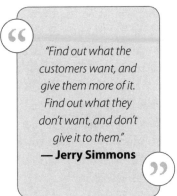

"Find out what the customers want, and give them more of it. Find out what they don't want, and don't give it to them."
— **Jerry Simmons**

Using the questions others have asked has both advantages and disadvantages. First, using existing questions saves time. Someone else has crafted the questions. They may have tested their questions to determine if they are asking what needs to be asked and will be understood by typical survey participants. If results are available, using the same questions provides an opportunity to benchmark responses in your organization against survey results from a larger sample.

A Caution Before Benchmarking

Sometimes we may want to see how our organization does when compared to other organizations. At times, such comparisons can be valuable. You can see how you measure up.

But such comparisons should be made with caution. Organizations are different. Circumstances are dissimilar. Sometimes, being above the multi-organizational benchmark may be something to celebrate. Sometimes it isn't. Exceeding the average by a few points may not be good enough for your organization.

On the other hand, questions created by someone else may not ask what you want to ask, or be asked in a way that they should be asked within your organization. Before using questions developed by someone else–including those in this book or at www.GREATstaffrecognition.com/bookbonus/surveyquestions–ensure that the questions are right for your situation. Your organization is different than others. What was a good question for them may not fit your organization's culture. Some questions may yield results that would be impossible to act on in your situation. There is no reason to ask about bonuses or extra time off if paying bonuses or giving time off would be in conflict with existing collective agreements or might violate legislative restrictions.

There is another rich source of input before preparing survey questions that is usually overlooked–people who will be responding to the survey. While it is impractical to gather input from the entire target group–that would be conducting a survey to conduct a survey—it is possible to collect valuable input from a few staff members who are representative of the population to be surveyed.

By listening to them, you will identify themes and issues related to recognition that are important to them. Survey questions can be used to explore these themes further. Questions that are focused on what staff feels is important can motivate more people to respond to the survey, and improve the overall quality of responses.

Open-ended Questions or Closed Questions?

Now that you know what you want to ask, you must next decide whether you will ask open-ended or closed questions. There are pros and cons associated with both types of questions.

Closed questions are those that require only a single response, such a number or a Yes/No answer. Closed questions also include multiple-choice questions. Responses to these questions provide a snapshot of how employees are feeling about recognition on the day when the questions were asked. Respondents can answer closed questions quickly and results can be tabulated quickly. Closed questions are best for determining how people feel about things as they are, but are less valuable in determining what to do to improve their satisfaction. What will be missing from the responses are any explanations that will help with interpretation of the responses. This information gap can lead to decisions based on assumptions about why respondents answered as they did. And we all know how often assumptions prove to be incorrect.

Open-ended questions can be more useful in learning how to improve how things are done. Open-ended questions require more of the respondents than checking a box or circling one of several suggested answers. These are the "short answer" questions of our school days, without the requirement to respond in complete sentences.

When answering open-ended questions, the respondents have more control of how the question is answered. They can use as many or as few words as they wish. They can provide explanations, share examples, or offer suggestions. There is greater richness in the information collected.

When answering open-ended questions, respondents may go in unexpected directions, revealing a diversity of ideas not available from responses to closed questions. Open-ended questions offer respondents the opportunity to discuss recognition-related topics and suggest modifications to recognition practices that the survey's author might not have imagined. Knowing that respondents will provide an explanation of their feelings about recognition, less wordsmithing may be required to develop questions that won't be misinterpreted. When answering open-end questions, respondents may provide insights into their interpretation of the question, which will make it easier to understand their responses.

Surveys based on open-ended questions will take longer for respondents to complete, which may have an adverse effect on response rates. They are not as easily "tabulated" as closed-ended questions, either.

Given the advantages and disadvantages associated with each type, those developing surveys often opt to include both open-ended and closed questions. Respondents are invited to add comments, either for each question or at the end of the survey.

"Here is Edward Bear coming downstairs now, bump, bump, on the back of his head behind Christopher Robin. It is, as far as he knows, the only way of coming downstairs, but sometimes he feels there really is another way, if only he could stop bumping for a moment and think about it."
— A. A. Milne, *author*

Do the Questions Work?

However you develop your survey questions, there is an additional step that, if taken, could increase the value of the responses you receive. Test your survey. Show it to others. Is the wording clear? Do others understand the questions as you understand them?

The testing process can be done during a series of meetings with individuals or with focus groups, during which five to 10 people who are similar to the group to be surveyed are asked to share their understanding of the questions. By taking time to test your questions, you can reduce the risk of semantic ambiguity that will confuse both respondents and those who will interpret the results. You have the opportunity to improve unclear questions and confusing directions.

Now that you have decided what you want to learn and written your questions, it is time to invite staff to complete your survey.

Before distributing the survey, let staff know it is coming through announcements, articles in internal newsletters, poster or emails. Explain why you are asking for their feedback and commit to act on what you find out. Tell them how the results of the survey will be shared and with whom. Will results be available to all staff or just to managers and supervisors? Will the complete results be released, or just a summary?

Distribute the survey to all staff, either in printed form or with a link to a website where the survey is available. Provide a deadline by which they should respond. To improve your response rate, plan to remind people to complete the survey as the deadline approaches.

If you are using a printed survey, consider providing an envelope. People seem to feel more anonymous when they can slip their completed survey into an envelope and seal it before submitting their input.

Online or On Paper?

Traditionally, surveys were printed on paper and completed with a pencil. Today, you have an alternative. There are several options available for affordable, easy-to-use web-based survey instruments that can be used instead of traditional paper and pencil surveys.

Before deciding between hardcopy and web-based surveys, there are pros and cons of each that should be considered:

Web-based – *Potential Advantages*
- Electronic surveys are environmentally sound. No paper is used.
- Web-based surveys are inexpensive or free, depending on the company used. Also, there are no photocopying costs.
- Respondents may feel a greater sense of anonymity.
- Responses are tabulated electronically and are available immediately.
- Written comments don't need to be transcribed. Simply cut and paste.
- Skip logic can be used to direct respondents through different paths in your survey based on responses to previous questions.

- Responses can be filtered, which enables you to look for specific data or patterns within the results, or cross-tabulated simply and quickly.
- Simple graphs can be created simply without you having to create spread sheets

Web-based – *Potential Disadvantages*
- Access to computers may be limited in some workplaces.
- Some people don't trust computers. They are worried that someone will be able to monitor their responses.
- Information is sent to a third-party server, often located in a foreign country.
- Depending on the settings you choose, respondents may not be able to look over the survey before beginning to answer the questions, or return to a previous question to modify or add to their answers.

Paper and Pencil – *Potential Advantages*
- Surveys can be administered to a group at the same time, such as during a staff meeting, which can increase response rates.
- Some respondents are more comfortable with a survey they can hold in their hands.
- Respondents can "thumb through" the survey before beginning to answer it and can easily return to previous questions to modify or add to their answers.
- Respondents may add comments and explanations that will be useful when interpreting results.

Paper and Pencil – *Potential Disadvantages*
- It takes time and expense to copy, distribute and collect surveys.
- Some respondents way worry that "someone will recognize my handwriting."
- It takes time to tabulate responses.
- Time is required to transcribe responses to open-ended questions.
- Spread sheets must be created before data can be presented as graphs.

Visit www.GREATstaffrecognition.com/bookbonus/websurveys for list of no-cost, low-cost web-based survey tools.

After the Survey

Once the deadline has passed, surveys should be tabulated and results made available as soon as possible. A review of the survey results may lead to obvious conclusions about what needs to happen to improve how staff is recognized. Often the results will point to many actions, more than can be undertaken at one time. An important part of survey followup is to decide which issues will be addressed first. Even though every concern will not be addressed right away, staff will see that something is happening. This builds trust for the survey process. Their opinions were not expressed in vain.

Surveys can often result in more questions than answers. More work will be required to decipher the meaning of what was discovered through the survey. Others can assist in this task, including other managers and supervisors. Front-line staff can also contribute to interpreting the results and proposing action.

> "Good companies tell you how they collect employee suggestions. Great companies tell you how they use them."
> — **Harvard Business Review**

Supervisors should share results with staff and ask, "What do you think this means? What does it tell us we should do?" These questions may lead to a lively discussion and debate that can define how to move forward and improve how staff is recognized.

At Least 13 Survey Questions You Might Use

Do you Agree or Disagree with the following statements
(1 = Strongly Disagree; 7 = Strongly Agree)

1. I feel appreciated for doing my job well.
   ❑ 1   ❑ 2   ❑ 3   ❑ 4   ❑ 5   ❑ 6   ❑ 7

2. It is important to me that I receive regular and frequent feedback on my work.
   ❑ 1   ❑ 2   ❑ 3   ❑ 4   ❑ 5   ❑ 6   ❑ 7

3. My supervisor knows and cares what is important to me.
   ❑ 1   ❑ 2   ❑ 3   ❑ 4   ❑ 5   ❑ 6   ❑ 7

4. The recognition I receive is aligned with the goals and values of the organization.
   ❏ 1   ❏ 2   ❏ 3   ❏ 4   ❏ 5   ❏ 6   ❏ 7

5. The recognition I receive is focused on what I need to do to do my job well.
   ❏ 1   ❏ 2   ❏ 3   ❏ 4   ❏ 5   ❏ 6   ❏ 7

6. Recognition is given to the most deserving individuals and groups.
   ❏ 1   ❏ 2   ❏ 3   ❏ 4   ❏ 5   ❏ 6   ❏ 7

7. I am recognized in ways that are meaningful to me.
   ❏ 1   ❏ 2   ❏ 3   ❏ 4   ❏ 5   ❏ 6   ❏ 7

8. The reasons for which I am being recognized are made clear to me.
   ❏ 1   ❏ 2   ❏ 3   ❏ 4   ❏ 5   ❏ 6   ❏ 7

9. From whom do you prefer to receive recognition
   (rank in order of preference, with 1 highest)
   _____ My immediate supervisor
   _____ A senior executive
   _____ Co-workers
   _____ Customers

10. From whom do you receive recognition most frequently
    (rank in order of frequency, with 1 the most frequent)
    _____ My immediate supervisor
    _____ A senior executive
    _____ Co-workers
    _____ Customers

11. Which do you receive more of at work?
    ❏ Praise   ❏ Criticism   ❏ Neither   ❏ Both equally

12. Do you prefer to be recognized in public (in front of co-workers or others) or in private (one-on-one)?
    ❏ Public   ❏ Private   ❏ No Preference

13. People have different preferences with respect to the form of recognition they would like to receive for doing a good job. Please indicate how you prefer to be recognized (check up to four).

❏ Cash bonus
❏ Small gift
❏ Email message of thanks
❏ Time off
❏ Article in the staff newsletter
❏ Announcement of my contribution or achievement at a staff meeting
❏ Acknowledgement by a co-worker
❏ Note of commendation placed in my personnel file
❏ Letter from my supervisor
❏ A few words of thanks from my supervisor
❏ A plaque or certificate of accomplishment
❏ Handwritten thank-you note
❏ Letter from my supervisor's boss
❏ Being nominated for a company-wide award
❏ Other (please specify) _____

For additional staff survey questions, visit www.GREATstaffrecognition.com/bookbonus/surveyquestions.

Appendix A
Create Your Own Staff Recognition Tool Kit

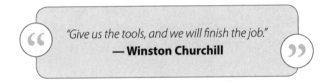

"Give us the tools, and we will finish the job."
— Winston Churchill

Having the right tools and having them ready to begin a job is what distinguishes a skilled tradesperson from a well-intentioned amateur. As someone skilled in staff recognition, you should ensure that you have the right tools available when they are needed. Here are some of the things to include as you assemble your Staff Recognition Tool Kit:

A collection of staff recognition techniques – a source of inspiration and variety for your recognition efforts. This book is a good starting point, but there are other books out there, including these three: *A Carrot a Day: A Daily Dose of Recognition for your Employees* by Adrian Gostick and Chester Elton; *Recognize and Reward Employees* by Donna Deeprose; and *101 Recognition Secrets: Tools for Motivating and Recognizing Today's Workforce* by Rosalind Jeffries. For more sources of staff recognition ideas, see Appendix B or visit www.GREATstaffrecognition.com/tipsandtechniques.

Recognition ball – a soft sponge-like ball that you use to encourage peer recognition by adding a recognition bounce to your staff meetings. See page 132 for instructions on the proper use of a recognition ball.

Recognition counters – pebbles, bingo markers, coins or poker chips—anything you can use to keep track of your daily recognition efforts. Begin your day with five objects in one pocket and move one to another pocket each time you recognize someone. If, at the end of the day, you have moved all five counters you have had a successful recognition day.

Thank-you cards – the most important tool for any staff recognition practitioner. Always have thank-you notes with you: on your desk, in your briefcase. Whenever you have a moment (waiting for an appointment, on an airplane, etc.), spend the time expressing your appreciation in writing. Supplement your supply of thank-you cards with greetings cards expressing other positive messages: welcome, congratulations or well done.

Sticky notes – a way to make the message of appreciation stick, to a computer screen, a desk, a report, in only a few words. When you reserve a distinct colour or shape of sticky note just for recognition purposes, recipients will know that you are expressing appreciation before they even read your words.

A pen – ideally with an ink colour, such as green or purple, that is only used for recognition. But remember that some colours can send messages that may conflict with your intention of expressing gratitude: black is the colour of photocopies, and we all recall from our school days the messages conveyed by our teachers' red pens.

Pass-along award – almost anything will work as this tool for peer recognition: a discarded sports trophy, a stuffed toy or something themed to your business. See page 129-130 for instructions on how to create and use a pass-along award.

Noise Maker – a horn or a bell, or something else to signal that someone is about to be recognized and to call staff together to celebrate the event.

Happy face stickers – attach a sticker when a staff member does something that makes you smile.

Banners – with various messages such as welcome, congratulations, happy birthday, to display at appropriate times.

Recognition Coupons – for on-the-spot recognition, providing small rewards to acknowledge an individual's contributions. Include space for a specific description of what was done and identification of what the recipient can redeem it for (an extended lunch break, restaurant gift certificate, a free coffee or snack, theatre tickets, the opportunity to leave an hour early at the end of the day, a car wash, lunch with the boss, free video rental, etc.) Coupons help make recognition make recognition **Appropriate** and **Timely.**

Presented to:	Presented to:
_____	in appreciation of:
(date)	_____
In appreciation of:	_____
_____	and may be redeemed for:
_____	_____
May be redeemed for:	_____
_____	(signature of presenter)
	_____
	(date)

Visit www. GREATstaffrecognition.com/bookbonus/coupon to print your own staff recognition coupons.

Learn More About Staff Recognition from the Experts

> *"There are as many ways to recognize people as there are people to recognize. You just have to use your brain to find them, the next time you think you've exhausted the possibilities, THINK AGAIN…and again!"*
> — **Eric Harvey,** *author*

While I would like to think that you will have learned everything you would want or need to know from me, my dog and all those other unlikely sources of insight and inspiration I've told you about, I know this is not going to be the case. There's lots more to learn about staff recognition and there are experts who offer different views of staff recognition. I encourage you to read what some of them have written. Any of these books will expand your recognition vision.

How Full is Your Bucket? Positive Strategies for Work and Life
by Tom Rath and Donald O. Clifton
(Gallup Press, 2004) ISBN 1 - 59562-003-6

From a lifetime of research by Clifton, a former chairman of The Gallup Organization, this book is based on the principle that everyone has an invisible bucket of self-esteem. We are at our best when our buckets are overflowing, and in every interaction we can either fill the buckets of others through positive words and actions, or dip from the bucket's level by being negative. As we fill the buckets of others we also fill our own.

Motivating People (Second Edition)
by Dayle M. Smith
(Hauppauge, NY: Barron's Educational Series, Inc., 1997) ISBN 0812098986.

This slim volume summarizes key research and theories about what motivates people, with suggestions on how to use the information. The central message is that different people are motivated by different things.

A Culture of Recognition: Building a System to Celebrate Great Performances
by Rhonda K. Sunnarborg
(Minneapolis, MN: Schoeneckers, Inc., 2000) ISBN 0967772311.

A guide for the design and operation of a recognition system which, unlike a recognition program, demonstrates a long-term commitment to recognition based on what the organization values.

1001 Ways to Reward Employees (Revised, Updated Edition)
by Bob Nelson
(New York: Workman Publishing Company Inc., 2005) ISBN 0761136819

This update of the staff recognition classic is filled with examples of what organizations have done to recognize and reward staff as individuals and teams. Examples run the gamut from no-cost to expensive, from informal to formal, from tangible to intangible. Throughout the book, the margins are filled with recognition tips and quotes. A third edition is scheduled to be pubished in late 2011 or early 2012.

You Made My Day: Creating Co-Worker Recognition and Relationships
by Janis Allen and Michael McCarthy
(New York: Lebhar-Friedman Books, 2000) ISBN 0867307870

The authors demonstrate how by encouraging peers to recognize their co-workers, organizations significantly increase the amount of recognition employees receive.

Make Their Day! Employee Recognition That Works
by Cindy Ventrice
(San Francisco, CA: Berrett-Koehler Publishers, Inc., 2003) ISBN 157675197X

Effective recognition is something that occurs every day, not at special events and through special awards. The author identifies four essential elements of effective recognition: praise, thanks, opportunity and respect, and provides advice to develop and use recognition practices that are meaningful and practical.

Encouraging the Heart: A Leader's Guide to Rewarding and Recognizing Others
by James M. Kouzes and Barry Z. Posner
(San Francisco, CA: Jossey-Bass, 2003) ISBN 0787964638

This book is based on the premise that people have a basic need to be appreciated for who they are and what they do. Unfortunately, expressions of appreciation are rare in many workplaces, despite evidence that when managers express appreciation performance improves. The authors identify seven essential components that are necessary to "encourage the heart," illustrated with real-life examples and hard data that demonstrates that they work.

The 1001 Rewards and Recognition Fieldbook
by Bob Nelson
(New York: Workman Publishing Company Inc., 2003) ISBN 0761121390

Likely the most comprehensive book on the subject, filled with tips, quotations, research, articles, forms and worksheets. This resource provides everything you need to plan, implement and evaluate your staff recognition program, whether formal or informal, focused on individuals or teams, well-funded or recognition-on-a-budget.

Love 'Em or Lose 'Em: Getting Good People to Stay (3rd Edition)
by Beverly Kaye and Sharon Jordan-Evans
(San Francisco, CA: Berrett-Koehler Publishers, Inc., 2005) ISBN 1576753271

Twenty-six chapters (From A for Ask to Z for Zenith) filled with strategies to avoid losing your best people. Each chapter topic corresponds to a letter of the alphabet, focusing on a different aspect of staff retention.

Anything by Adrian Gosick and Chester Elton, who seem to turn out a book a year, including:

Managing with Carrots:
Using Recognition to Attract and Retain the Best People
(Salt Lake City, UT: Gibbs Smith Publishers, 2001) ISBN 1586580776

The 24-Carrot Manager:
A Remarkable Story of How a Leader Can Unleash Human Potential
(Salt Lake City, UT: Gibbs Smith Publishers, 2002) ISBN 1586581543

A Carrot a Day: A Daily Dose of Recognition for Your Employees
(Salt Lake City, UT: Gibbs Smith Publishers, 2004) ISBN 1586855069

The Carrot Principle:
How the Best Managers Use Recognition to Engage Their People,
Retain Talent, and Accelerate Performance
(New York: Free Press, A Division of Simon & Schuster, Inc., 2007)
ISBN 9780743290098

The Daily Carrot Principle:
365 Ways to Enhance Your Career and Life
(New York: Free Press, A Division of Simon & Schuster, Inc., 2010)
ISBN 9781439181737

The Orange Revolution:
How One Great Team Can Transform an Entire Organization
(New York: Free Press, A Division of Simon & Schuster, Inc., 2010)
ISBN 9781439182451

Notes

Introduction: It All Started With a Single Question

Page 2

"In research first conducted by Lawrence Lindahl in 1949…"

Information related to Lawrence Lindahl's original research and its replication in the 1980s, 1990s and 2001, was found in the following:

- Paul Hersey and Kenneth H. Blanchard. *Management of Organizational Behavior: Utilizing Human Resources, 5th edition.* Englewood Cliffs: Pentice Hall, 1988.
- Dayle M. Smith. *Motivating People.* Hauppauge, NY: Barron's Education Service, Inc. 1997.
- Helen Straughn. "Employee Retention," http://www.apco911.org/institute/emd_pdf/EmployeeRetention.pdf

Page 5

"An examination of psychologist Abraham Maslow's 'hierarchy of needs'…"

Information on Maslow's hierarchy of needs was found in the following:

- Anne Bruce and James S. Pepitore. *Managing People.* Toronto: McGraw-Hill,1999.
- Nancy Langton and Stephen P. Robins. *Organizational Behaviour.* Toronto: Pearson Prentice Hall, 2007.

- Albrahm H. Maslow. *Motivation and Personality, 2nd edition.* New York: Harper and Row, 1970.
- Dayle M. Smith. *Motivating People.* Hauppauge, NY: Barron's Education Service, Inc. 1997.

Chapter 1: Paved With Good Intentions

Page 25
"A study by the Cornell University Institute for Health and Productivity suggests that sick people..."

Information comes from a news release from Cornell University, dated April 20, 2004, *"Economists coin new word, 'presenteeism,' to describe worker slowdowns that account for up to 60 percent of employer health costs"* (http://www.news.cornell.edu/releases/April04/cost.illness.jobs.ssl.html)

Chapter 2: The 5 Ingredients that Make Staff Recognition GREAT

Page 35
"The Dave Brubeck Quartet was getting a lot of radio time with its newly-released *Take Five*..."

Information related to Take Five was drawn from an Wikipedia entry entitled, *"Take Five"* (http://en.wikipedia.org/wiki/Take_Five)

Chapter 4: Mission Misunderstood = Mission Impossible

Page 49
"Groups that have high scores on this item were more productive..."

- Rodd Wagner and James K. Harter. 12: *The Elements of Great Managing* Washington, DC: The Gallup Organization, 2006, pp. 3-4.

Chapter 7: Recognition Delayed is Recognition Diminished

Page 75
"Some time ago, a teacher with whom I worked was nominated for an Excellence in Teaching Award…"

The timeline for Excellence in Teaching Award has been changed so that the awards are now presented before the end of the same school year in which the nominations are submitted.

Excuses, Rationalizations and Cop-outs (Part II)

Page 80
"Nearly two-thirds of those surveyed …"

Tom Rath and Donald O. Clifton. *How Full Is Your Bucket? Positive Strategies for Work and Life.* New York: Gallup Press, 2004

Chapter 9: Once is Never Enough

Page 101
"Research by The Gallup Organization identified 12 survey questions that, when answered in the affirmative…:

The 12 questions are discussed in two books:

- Marcus Buckingham and Curt Coffman. *First, Break all the Rules: What the World's Greatest Managers Do Differently.* New York: Simon and Shuster, 1999
- Rodd Wagner and James K. Harter. *12: The Elements of Great Managing.* Washington, DC: The Gallup Organization, 2006

Page 102

"Gallup found that people who don't feel appreciated are less engaged…"

Rodd Wagner and James K. Harter. *12: The Elements of Great Managing.* Washington, DC: The Gallup Organization, 2006

"This appears to be particularly true for younger workers…"

The recognition needs of members of different generations is discussed in the following:

- Lynne C. Lancaster and David Stillman, *When Generations Collide.* (New York: Harper Collins, 2002).
- Michael McQueen, *The 'New' Rules of Engagement: A Guide to Understanding and Connecting with Generation Y.* (Greenwich, Australia: The Nextgen Group, 2011).

Chapter 10: Money Don't Buy You Much These Days… and Likely Never Could

Page 106

"A study by American Express Incentive Services found…"

Cited by Adrian Gostick and Chester Elton in *Managing with Carrots: Using Recogntion to Attract and Retain the Best People.* Laynton, Utah: Gibbs Smith, 2001.

Chapter 12: In the Words of Others

Page 121

"Researchers suggest that 60 per cent of all conversations…"

Based on personal conversation with PhD candidate Shawne Duperon about her research.

Chapter 13: Trust Recognition to Those Who Know Best

Page 136

"Staff recognition needs the equivalent of 360-degrees appraisal systems…"

360-degree appraisal is discussed by Gary Dessler and Nina D. Cole in *Human Resource Management in Canada*. Toronto: Pearson Prentice Hall, 2008.

Chapter 15: Punished for Success

Page 150

"A recent study by Leadership IQ found that the very people who make organizations successful…"

A summary of this study is available at www.leadershipiq.com/quitting.html.

Chapter 16: What I Learned from Dan's Mother

Page 159

"At its annual convention that year, the National Speakers' Association presented…"

The Cavett, named in honour of National Speakers Association founder Cavett Roberts, is the association's highest honour, awarded once annually to an individual whose lifetime work is exemplary.

Chapter 20: Funerals for the Living

Page 175

"A few days after U.S. Senator Edward Kennedy was diagnosed with brain cancer…"

This conversation occurred during the May 25, 2008 broadcast of NBC's *Meet the Press*.

Chapter 21: Hug People, Not Your Computer

Page 185
"In the 1980s, author and management consultant Tom Peters…"

Audrey C. Daniels makes reference to Management by Walking Around in *Bring Out the Best in People*. Toronto: McGraw-Hill, 2000.

Chapter 23: How Green is Staff Recognition

Page 197
"Bob Nelson…estimates that $27 billion is spent annually on recognition merchandise."

Bob Nelson supplied this estimate in response to an inquiry from the author.

Chapter 28: Hire Recognizers and Those Who Been Recognized

Page 246
"This question is written in a behaviour description interview style…"

Behaviour Description Interviewing and similar approaches to interviewing are described in the following:

- Lori Davila and Louis Kursmark. *How to Choose the Right Person for the Right Job Every Time*. New York: McGraw-Hill, 2005.
- Richard S. Deems. *Hiring: More Than a Gut Feeling*. Franklin Lakes, NJ: Career Press, 1995.
- Tom Janz, Lowell Hellervik, and David C. Gilmore. *Behavior Description Interviewing*. Toronto: Allyn and Bacon, Inc., 1986.

Acknowledgements

When I reflect back on the journey that was the writing of this book, I realize how many people touched the process and influenced the final product. Their support and advice were invaluable. Without them, this book likely would have remained a dream, a task on my long-term to-do list, and the source of the frustration associated with incomplete projects.

I begin by recognizing my friend and colleague Linda Maul who may have been the first to ask, "Where is the book?" and fellow Rotarian Christoph Wilser who would greet me each at each Tuesday morning by asking, "How is your book coming?"

Others shared their staff recognition experiences and techniques, which appear throughout the book. These include Linda Atchinson, Patti Sparks, Melissa Thompson, Kath Rhyason, Dianne Batstone, Robert Prather, Tamisan Benzc-Knight, May Harvie, Phil Meagher, Alice Cartwright and participants in my workshops and seminars.

Catherine Moir, Lisa Litwinski and Dan Ohler helped me discover the right title for the book.

When I needed specific information, there people to whom I could go. Lorn Stanners, David Kinnaird and Dr. Bob Nelson generously responded to my requests and willingly shared their knowledge and expertise.

Gina Fowler, Lorna Tollman, William Betteridge, Deidre Norris, Sharon Shultz, and Scott McDonald all read early drafts of several chapters and offered useful feedback.

Calgary-based speaker Kit Grant saw the potential that the words I used to describe the ingredients of meaningful staff recognition could form the acronym **GREAT—Genuine, Relevant, Explicit, Appropriate** and **Timely.**

Thank you to self-publishing guru Dan Poynter from what I learned from his books, workshops and personal conversations. Thanks also to Canadian Association of Professional Speakers colleagues Val Kinjerski, Jim Clemmer and Debbie Elicksen for their advice on writing, publishing and marketing books. And of course, there was the support of the CAPS Edmonton community—people who understand why people write books.

There was also the staff in the various Edmonton coffee shops where I spent time writing. They never hassled me or requested that I leave, despite that I would only purchase a cup of tea and an occasional bagel or muffin before occupying a table for hours.

An author's best friend and most trusted ally is his editor. For more than 18 months, Helen Metella read drafts of the manuscript, correcting typos and spelling errors, checking facts, offering advice, and generally improving how well the book read. Helen did her best to ensure my writing was coherent.

It's been nearly ten years since I first met Andrew Johnstone, who is responsible for how the book looks. And for most of this time, I have promised him that I would have a book for him to design "soon." I thank him for his patience and advice, as well as the quality of his book design. *Thanks! GREAT Job!* is not just a title. It reflects how I feel about what Andrew has done.

And finally, I must express appreciation to my wife June for her support and understanding during this decade-long project. She realized that writing this book is something I was driven to do and even accepted that "going on vacation" was simply code for escaping the daily routine so I could write. Parts of this book accompanied us to Europe, South America, Mexico, Alaska and throughout the Caribbean and the Baltic.

About the Author

Since becoming a full-time consultant, speaker, trainer and facilitator in 1995, Nelson Scott has worked with clients who are committed to hiring the right people, developing and retaining productive staff, and strengthening relationships with customers. He sees his presentations and writing as opportunities to remind audiences and readers what they already know and challenge them to build on this knowledge to make the right hiring decisions, recognize staff effectively and provide exceptional customer service.

Nelson has inspired public- and private-sector audiences across Western Canada. He is a former president of the Edmonton chapter of the Canadian Association of Professional Speakers and a member of the International Association of Facilitators and Recognition Professionals International.

Nelson's first career was a teacher in Fort McMurray, Alberta. He taught grades 4 to 6, was principal of an elementary school and, for 14 years, assistant superintendent. He has also taught business courses to college students.

Thanks! GREAT Job! is Nelson's first book, but others are in the works related to staff recognition, hiring interviews and customer service.

To contact Nelson, or schedule a presentation for your staff or association email nmscott@telus.net or phone (780) 433-1443.

Index

Order Form

To order additional copies of *Thanks! GREAT Job!*
- Fax this form to (780) 433-1413
- **Mail this form to:**
  SEA Consulting, 7243 – 112 Street, Edmonton, AB T6G 1J4, Canada
- Visit the bookstore at www.GREATstaffrecognition.com

Please send me the following number of copies of *Thanks! GREAT Job!*

Quantity	Cost	Total
	$20.00 per book	$
	Shipping & handling (first book):	$ 4.00
Shipping & handling (add $2.50 for each additional book):		$
	Subtotal:	$
	Canadian residents add 5% GST*:	$
	Total:	$

*GST #: 885169771

Shipping information:

Name: _____

Address: _____

_____

City:_____Province: _____ Postal Code: _____

Daytime phone number: _____

E-mail: _____

Payment information:

❑ cheque (Payable to SEA Consulting)   ❑ Visa   ❑ MasterCard

Card number: _____ Expiration: _____ / _____

Signature: _____

Please contact us for foreign orders and quantity discounts.